THE MODERN 1-4 BASKETBALL OFFENSE

An Attack for All Defenses

THE MODERN 1-4
BASKETBALL OFFENSE

An Attack for All Defenses

JOSEPH J. CERAVOLO

Parker Publishing Company, Inc., West Nyack, N.Y.

PRINTED IN THE UNITED STATES OF AMERICA
13-595926-8   BC

DEDICATION

TO: My wife, Dorothy
My three sons, Darryl, Robert, and Joey
My mother and father
My basketball players at Palm Beach High School

AND

IN MEMORY OF

Nate Lippe—Coach
George Deitz—Player
David Wilkerson—Manager

WHY I DECIDED TO WRITE THIS BOOK

For the last several years the offensive alignment used at Palm Beach High School has been the one-four (1-4). While we have been very successful over these years, our success was never attributed to our 1-4 alignment. Instead our winning was always traced to other factors such as superior personnel, luck, over-emphasis, officiating, and other reasons. Very few of our early critics linked our winning to this new concept of offensive play.

The realization that the 1-4 is the modern offense for all defenses was very slow in coming. Many times, prior to its full acceptance, I was chided by several of my colleagues. Now that it is being adopted by many teams across the country, the pains I once suffered during those pioneering days are rapidly being soothed.

Our 1-4 was born early in 1961. Like so many discoveries it, too, was conceived by accident.

We were a match-up zone defensive team, and we ran a 1-3-1 offense against most of the zone defenses we faced. One afternoon, my first team was practicing its match-up against the 1-3-1 offense of our second unit. As the offensive point man was putting the ball in play, the baseline man felt that it was time for him to get the ball and take a shot at the basket, just as his teammates had been doing for ten minutes or more. Because he hadn't been receiving the ball underneath or in the corners, he decided to break from his baseline position near the basket up to the side of the foul line. The point man happened to see him and passed him the ball. Much to his surprise, not to mention mine, he was wide open and had an uncontested shot from the foul line. He continued this maneuver and scored at will against a team that had already proven that it was a good defensive club.

When I was asked by my defensive players what adjustment they should make, I was stymied. Therefore, in order to save face for not coming up with a sound answer, I decided to incorporate the move into our offense. At the time, we just referred to the maneuver as our double post offense. After a little research I found that our double post offense wasn't really new and that it had been in use as far back as 1937. I also learned that this maneuver with one man out front and four men aligned across the floor extending from foul extended line to foul line extended was referred to by those who knew it as the 1-4.

Although we do not seek credit for discovery of the 1-4, we most certainly must be recognized as being one of the very first to employ it exclusively against all defenses.

Like most basketball coaches, I possess the burden of great indebtedness to our game. I am hoping that this presentation of the 1-4 will help pay back a fraction of the debt I owe to basketball.

JOE CERAVOLO

Special Gratitude

TO: My alma mater: Davis and Elkins College
My family: sisters, aunts, uncles, and cousins
My three good friends:

Robert D'Angio
Dr. Edward Eissey
Ralph Greco

My typist: Dorothy Ceravolo
My proofreader: Ralph Greco
My principals: John McDonald

Howard Swyers

My assistant coaches and managers
My coaches: Roger Jones, Aliquippa Junior High School

Nate Lippe, Aliquippa High School
Robert N. Brown, University of West Virginia
Peter (Press) Maravich, Louisiana State University
and
Dr. Glenn Wilkes, Stetson University

For making the publication possible

CONTENTS

11

Key to Diagrams

① ② ③ ④ ⑤   Offensive Players

X¹ X² X³ X⁴ X⁵   Defensive Players

-------→   Pass

∿∿∿→   Dribble

————⊣   Screen

· · · · · · · ·>   Shot

————→   Path of Player

❶ ❷ ❸ ❹ ❺   Players in Possession of Ball

1

THE ORIGIN AND ADVANTAGES

OF THE 1-4 OFFENSE

Origin and Development of the 1-4

With the advent of the jump shot, pressure defenses, and a more even distribution of big men among participating teams, basketball today is a totally different game than it was 25 years ago. In our game, the offense for some time now has been ahead of the defense and, furthermore, must remain so in order for the game as we know it to survive. Recently, however, discipline offenses coupled with new concepts of defensive play have dealt a severe blow to the big lead once enjoyed. Which of the two is more responsible for shortening this advantage is debatable. I like to think the new defensive thinking is effecting this change, rather than the slowed down, pass-up-the-good-shot, discipline offenses which in my opinion can only bring harm to the game's image. Coaches can cope with new systems of defensive play, but it is impossible to cope with no play. It is in line with this thinking that I offer the 1-4.

The new thinking in defensive play causing our problems today is away from the earlier concepts that man-to-man defensive teams cannot or should not play zone defense, and that zone teams should by no means play man-to-man. Defensive coaches who believe they can avoid playing more than one kind of defense are comparable to football coaches who stay in the 6-2-2-1 defense for an entire game. Yes, it can be done, but only by a team with a tremendous personnel advantage. Today, good defensive coaches constantly teach and practice sound man-to-man defensive principles. It matters little to them what defense they plan to use in a game or over an entire season. They realize that good man-to-man players make good zone players and pressure defensive people as well. It is because of this new thinking

17

that the 1-4 offense came into being. As I see it, the greatest threat to the offensive supremacy of the game is not head-to-head, hard-nose man-to-man defense or a quick sliding pinch of the middle type zones. A good offensive player will beat a good tight-playing defensive player consistently. Good passing and controlled set offensive teams with movement of their players will eventually force zone teams into giving up the good shot. The big threat comes from teams that:

1. Incorporate zone principles into their man-to-man defenses.
2. Use man-to-man and zone pressure defenses.
3. Use zone defenses with man-to-man principles.
4. Use various combinations of these defenses mentioned above.

Therefore, in order for the 1-4 to be a true attack for all defenses it must be effective against the straight man-to-man defenses, the various zones, and all possible combinations.

The use of man-to-man defense with zone principles has been going on for some time. Most man-for-man people have been employing a four-man sag toward the middle. They have been sagging the weak-side defensive forward or weak-side guard, two passes removed from the location of the ball, so that they can help out when the offensive man beats the defensive man. This type of defense has been highly successful. Recently, however, set offenses such as the many variations of the shuffle, wheel, and other controlled offenses have frequently been successful against them. The result has been that thinking coaches have initiated changes in their defense.

College coaches and high school coaches using controlled set of-fenses were the scourge of the country a few years ago, and many of them are still among the best in the country. But with the advent of pressure defenses where the offensive man is picked up early, over-played, and double-teamed it is becoming increasingly difficult to penetrate close enough to get the set offenses started.

To get set offenses started against such defenses necessitates plac-ing greater demands on the offensive abilities of the players. Whereas a few years ago we were able to play players who were poor dribblers, poor drivers, and poor one-on-one players, today, in my opinion, we cannot.

In beating pressure defenses the main responsibilities rest on the individual players' shoulders. Free-lance basketball players have more success against pressure than do controlled set offensive players. However, free-lance players have more difficulty against sagging man-to-man and zone defenses.

The answer is obvious: develop free-lance basketball players. Take their moves and make them the initial step in the development of a controlled offense. Now you have players who are capable of beating pressure defenses with their free-lance moves. With these moves incorporated into a controlled offense they are capable of beating sagging and zone defenses as well.

The starting point of an offense such as this is the development of the individual. Every player must be well-schooled in the fundamentals of shooting, one-on-one moves, driving, passing, rebounding, screening, and dribbling. Furthermore, the coach must have a controlled offensive pattern that is initiated at the start of a player's shot: drive, pass, rebound, screen, and dribble. Almost all coaches teach good sound offensive fundamentals, and almost all coaches have developed great individual players. Today, almost every team has at least one or two really good players who are the products of their coaching. However, very few coaches have drawn up controlled offenses initiated by the fundamentals they teach. This is a relatively easy task, and one which can be accomplished by almost any experienced coach. It can be done from any of a number of alignments—the 2-3, 1-3-1, and 1-2-2 as well as the 1-4.

Definition of the 1-4

The 1-4 offense is more an alignment than an offense. Initially the alignment was used strictly to combat zone defenses, but as the defenses became more numerous and more complex I decided to use it against all defenses. I was once one of those coaches who attacked man-to-man sagging teams with one kind of offense, zones with a different offense, and pressure defenses with a third or fourth offense. I spent more time during the course of the game trying to figure out the opposing team's defense than on any other phase of the game. My kids were spending more time trying to read defenses than they were spending on trying to free themselves to score. The result was that I became confused and so did my players. To cope with all defenses, my need for one kind of offense became apparent.

Our 1-4 is a controlled free-lance offense. I believe that the best basketball can be played only when the offensive player can force the defensive man into making a mistake and then effectively capitalizing upon it. He must not have any preconceived thoughts as to what this movement will be but must let the defensive man dictate his action. He must evaluate each situation and react accordingly. He must never become mechanical or stereotyped.

It is the job of the coach to take the various reactions a player can make and organize them so that the four remaining players can be brought into play in a smooth and controlled manner.

I predict that the true value of the 1-4 offense will eventually prove comparable to the T-Formation and do for basketball what the latter did for single winged football.

The 1-4 Alignment

Our 1-4 offense consists of two different alignments. They are the deep 1-4, illustrated in Figure 1-1, and the normal 1-4 alignment, illustrated in Figure 1-2.

In Figure 1-1 all four line players are aligned along the baseline. All of the plays that we will outline will be diagramed from the normal 1-4 alignment (Figure 1-2). However, all of the plays to be diagramed for your consideration could have been drawn up from the deep 1-4 alignment as well.

The Point Man

The point position is a rather fluid position. It is true that it is to our advantage for the point man to be able to bring the ball up the court to the top of the key; however, many times he is forced to the left or to the right of the top of the circle. Figure 1-3 shows the range of the point position.

The point man has to be the complete basketball player. He must be smart, alert, quick, possess a good understanding of the game, and have a thorough knowledge of and complete confidence in your system of play. He must be capable of picking out the flaws in the opposing team's defense, taking into account mismatches against the zones and the personal foul status of the various defensive players.

He must be an excellent passer. Since he puts the ball in play each time down the court, he must be able to execute with accuracy the following passes: chest pass, baseball pass, two-handed overhead pass, and bounce pass. He must be able to perfect these passes toward a stationary target as well as toward moving targets. He must be a great

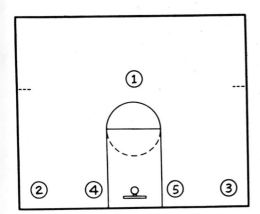

Figure 1-1

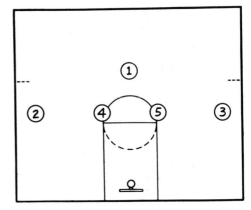

Figure 1-2

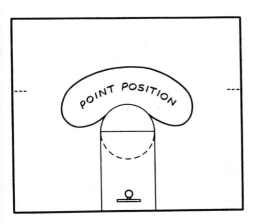

Figure 1-3

dribbler. He must be capable of controlling the ball and the defender as he brings the ball up court against any one defensive man. He must be able to pass quickly off the dribble to the open man when double-teamed, and able to beat the double team when in trouble. He must be a good outside shooter. He must be able to shoot off the dribble and behind a screener. Along with being a good driver, he must possess all of the various one-on-one moves. Finally, he must be able to play the wing position as well.

The Pivotmen

The pivotmen play a position just to the side of the foul line. We ask our pivotmen to place their feet above the foul line and straddle the black line that marks the beginning of the circle with their inside foot.

Both pivotmen must be big strong rebounders, good feeders, good shooters, and good drivers. They must be capable of setting good screens at the point, wing, corner, and off-side pivot positions. Figures 1-4 and 1-5 illustrate these screening areas.

Furthermore, after screening, the pivotmen must be able to roll toward the basket. They must recognize when the mismatch has occurred and be able to score consistently against the smaller defender. They must be able to score one-on-one with their backs to the basket. They must possess all of the one-on-one moves facing the basket. Finally, they must be good tippers.

The Wing Men

The wing men at times must play the point position. Therefore, the more complete basketball players they are the more an asset they will be in the 1-4. The wing men must be good one-on-one players as well as good drivers. They must be a threat from 15 to 18 feet away from the basket. They must be able to shoot behind a screen and work off the pivotman. They should be adequate passers, dribblers, and re-bounders.

Advantages and Disadvantages of the 1-4 Offense

The advantages of the 1-4 are varied and numerous, and it is not my intention to outline a long, impressive list of them. I will confine myself to those that I feel are a definite advantage over the more conventional types of offenses, such as the 2-3, the 1-2-2, and the 1-3-1. The advantages of the 1-4 can be broken down and classified into these three main categories:

   a. More versatility in the use of offensive personnel.
   b. Better rebounding.
   c. The cause of more defensive problems to the opposition.

The 1-4 allows a coach to enjoy more versatility in the use of his personnel because:

   1. It permits him to use two big men in the pivot position. Many teams have two big boys that they would like to use at one time. However, more times than not neither one is able to make the necessary adjustments to play the forward position. The 1-4 solves such a predicament. It now gives the coach two big men

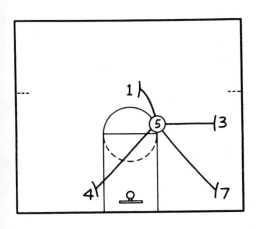

Figure 1-4

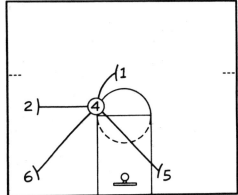

Figure 1-5

instead of only one and allows both to play up close to the basket.

2. It permits the coach to play with one little man, two larger forwards, and two centers. To play with only one little man makes it possible for a coach to have that extra height in the ball game at one time.

3. It permits him to play with three guards and two centers. Many times during the course of a ball game it is to the coach's advantage to have a little extra speed in the lineup for pressing and for fast break purposes, or for better ball handling so necessary for the control-type game. The 1-4 with the three guard, two center combination satisfies this need without sacrificing or changing your offense to any extent.

4. It permits him to play with two guards, one forward, and two centers if needed.

Among the various reasons why 1-4 teams enjoy a rebounding advantage are the following factors:

1. The mere fact that two big men can play at one time most certainly will increase the team's rebounding strength.

2. The 1-4 permits all off-side rebounding to be handled by a center rather than by the off-side forward.

3. It takes less time for the offensive rebounders to get to their rebounding areas on shots taken from the point or wing positions.

Probably the greatest argument for using the 1-4 is that it creates the following defensive problems for the opposing team:

1. It forces the opposition to cover the pivot area with two people, one of whom has less experience defending a pivotman than the other. Most teams are used to defending the pivot with their center. Against the 1-4 one of their forwards must also be schooled in defending the pivot area.

2. It takes away from the defense many trapping opportunities. With a one-guard front the defense cannot trap out front unless they leave one of the wing men free for an abnormal length of time.

3. It is more difficult to defend a single point man than it is to defend a guard as part of a two-man front. Against a two-man

front, the off-side defensive guard helps to shut off the drive toward the middle. There is no off-side defensive guard defending against the 1-4.

4. It forces zone teams into playing man-to-man defenses. (This is to be discussed at length in a later chapter.)

The 1-4 is by no means without some disadvantages. There are two important ones that its coach must be aware of:

1. It requires specific personnel.
2. It places limitations on your defense.

By now you are aware that it takes two big men to play the center positions in the 1-4. Many times it is difficult enough to find one big man who can play. The 1-4 may now double the problem the coach has in his constant pursuit of big people. 1-4 teams may suffer defensively from two big people in the lineup at one time. It is more difficult to use pressing defenses because most big men do not react quickly enough to make full-court or half-court presses effective. As the development of the 1-4 unfolds in the chapters that follow, I am confident that coaches will be conscious of the marked effect it will have on the various defenses being used today. I am hopeful that once it is presented and fully understood you will agree that *the 1-4 is the modern offense against all defenses.*

2

DEVELOPING

THE 1-4 MULTIPLE OFFENSE

There are three major problems that must be contended with in order for us to develop the 1-4 offense into a multiple offense capable of combating all types of defenses. They are:

1. The offense must be able to cope successfully with all types of sagging man-to-man defenses.
2. The offense must be able to combat all types of zone defenses.
3. The offense must be able to defeat pressure man-to-man and pressure zone defenses.

We believe, as stated earlier, that the solution to all of these problems basically, rests with the development of the individual into a good free-lance basketball player. Once this is accomplished, take his moves and make them the initial step in the development of a controlled offense. Here we will concern ourselves with the development of the 1-4 offense to combat sagging man-to-man defenses. Solutions to problems 2 and 3 will be discussed in Chapters 10 and 14.

Since free-lance moves belong to the players, and if we are going to utilize their moves in our offense, our offense should be developed by the players themselves. This is exactly the way our offense is constructed—every phase of it is constructed by the players under our leadership and guidance. The approach we use to develop such an offense begins with our taking a basketball and giving it to one of our point men at the head of the key. We construct our offense by asking the point man a question and developing his answers into rules.

The question we ask the point man is: What can you do when you have possession of the ball? After thinking a moment, he will come up with the following:

1. When I am in possession of the ball, I can pass it.
2. When I am in possession of the ball, I can dribble it.
3. When I am in possession of the ball, I can shoot it.
4. When I am in possession of the ball, I can drive to the basket.

The conclusion is that since there isn't anything else constructive that a player in possession of the ball can do, we must have plays that are initiated by a pass, a dribble, a drive, and a shot. With plays that are so initiated, the point man in this system cannot possibly make a mistake. If the point man has time to come down the floor and look the situation over, he can deliberately decide to run a particular play based upon his critical analysis of the defense (an example of the control game). On the other hand he can come down the floor with the ball and be forced to respond quickly, even instinctively, to a given situation by using one of his four alternatives (an example of the free-lance game). In both cases he is able to cope successfully with the defense by initiating a play. Both situations can be handled without fear of making some kind of offensive mistake.

After the question asked the point man has been answered, we can then begin to develop the offense from any one of his alternatives—pass, dribble, shoot, and drive. Before we do, I believe it is time to point out some of the qualities we want our 1-4 offense to contain. For the 1-4 to be able to attack all defenses successfully we are primarily concerned with the development of the following qualities:

1. The offense must contain good offensive rebounding.
2. The offense must be simple to execute.
3. The offense must consist of as few play patterns as possible.
4. Collectively the play patterns selected must be able to combat all types of defenses.
5. Each play pattern must have several options.
6. Each play pattern must be initiated from a free-lance move.
7. We must be able to incorporate the free-lance moves into a controlled offense consisting of team movement and quick-passes.

Development of the 1-4 Offense from a Pass

With the point man in possession of the ball, we pursue our questioning of him one step further. The second question we ask of him would be: Once in possession of the ball to whom could you pass?

The answer would be to either one of the two wing men or to either one of the two centers (Figure 2-1).

At this point it is time for the coach to introduce to the squad the following two rules that will govern their play:

RULE 1: After passing the ball to a teammate, move to a new floor position.

RULE 2: After receiving the ball from your teammate, play with the man who passes you the ball.

The following is a list of all the movements point man 0-1 can make after passing the ball to wing man 0-2:

1. Pass and cut clear to the opposite side (Route 1, Figure 2-2).

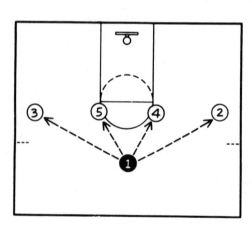

Figure 2-1

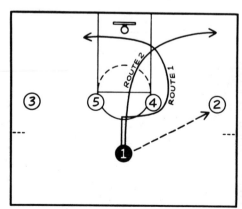

Figure 2-2

2. Pass and cut to the corner on the same side of the court as the ball (Route 2, Figure 2-2).
3. Pass and screen toward the ball in front of 0-2 (Figure 2-3).
4. Pass and cut toward the ball going behind 0-2 (Figure 2-3).
5. Pass and screen away from the ball for wing man 0-3 (Figure 2-4).
6. Pass and screen for pivotman 0-5 (Figure 2-5).

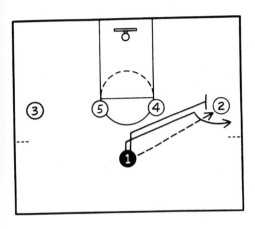

Figure 2-3

Figure 2-4

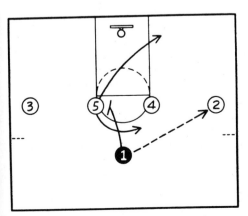

Figure 2-5

7. Pass and screen for pivotman 0-4 (Figure 2-6).

All of the possible movements that 0-1 can make after passing the ball to 0-2 have been exhausted.

With 0-2 abiding by Rule 2: (play with the man who throws you the ball) 0-1 can make any of the movements illustrated and 0-2 will play with him. In Figures 2-2 and 2-3, 0-2 could return the ball to 0-1. In Figure 2-4, 0-2 could pass the ball to 0-3. In Figure 2-5, 0-2 could pass the ball to 0-5. In Figure 2-6, 0-2 could pass the ball to 0-4.

In every case, however, once the ball is passed by 0-2, 0-2 must abide by Rule 1. That means he must move to a new position after passing. In each play after he passes the ball, he must answer the question, "What can I do after passing the ball?" In Figure 2-2, if 0-2 passes the ball to 0-1 he must follow the ball and become a rebounder.

In Figure 2-2, after 0-1 goes to the corner 0-2 has the following opportunities (Figure 2-7):

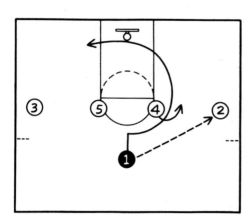

Figure 2-6

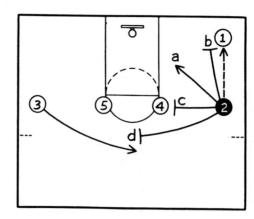

Figure 2-7

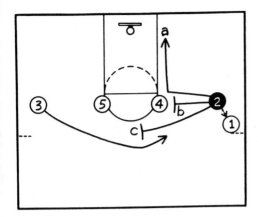

Figure 2-8

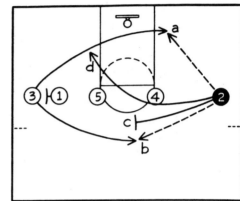

Figure 2-9

a. He can pass to 0-1 and cut for the basket.
b. He can screen toward the ball for 0-1.
c. He can screen away from the ball for 0-4.
d. He can screen for 0-3 away from the ball.

In Figure 2-3, after 0-1 goes behind 0-2, and 0-2 hands him the ball, 0-2 has the following opportunities (Figure 2-8):

a. 0-2 can cut to the basket.
b. 0-2 can screen for 0-4.
c. 0-2 can screen away from the ball for 0-3.

In Figure 2-4, 0-2 has the following opportunities (Figure 2-9):

a. 0-2 can pass to 0-3 under the basket.
b. 0-2 can pass to 0-3 at the top of the key.
c. 0-2 can pass to 0-3 and screen.
d. 0-2 can pass to 0-3 at the top of key and make a shuffle cut to the basket.

31

In Figure 2-5, 0-2 has the following opportunities (Figure 2-10):

a. Pass the ball to 0-5 under the basket and follow the ball.

b. Pass the ball to 0-5 at the top of the key and screen for 0-5.

c. Pass the ball to 0-5 at the top of the key and make a shuffle cut off 0-4 to the basket.

In Figure 2-6, 0-2 has the following opportunities after 0-1 sets a running screen for 0-4 (Figure 2-11):

a. Pass the ball to 0-1.

b. Pass the ball to 0-4.

c. Pass the ball to 0-3 and screen for 0-3.

d. Pass the ball to 0-3 and make a shuffle cut to the basket.

The point man and the wing man have exhausted all of the possibilities afforded them that can be made from a pass to the wing men. All of our diagrams have been drawn up based on pass to our right wing player 0-2. These same diagrams can be duplicated on the left side of the floor whenever the point man passes the ball to our left wing player 0-3. The only other passing opportunity that the point man can make is a pass to the pivotman (Figure 2-12).

Once the point man passes the ball to 0-4, he must move. Again he is questioned as to what movements he can make. The following is a list of practical movements 0-1 can make after passing to 0-4, each of which is illustrated in Figure 2-12:

1. A cut off pivotman 0-4.
2. A screen for wing man 0-2.
3. A screen for wing man 0-3.
4. A screen for pivotman 0-5.

This concludes our discussion of developing the 1-4 offense from a pass by the point man to a teammate. In this short discussion we have presented over 70 scoring opportunities just by having the point man pass the ball and by adherence to rules 1 and 2.

The Development of the 1-4 Offense from a Dribble

The dribble as we use it is employed by our team members as a means of replacing a pass. We do not use the term dribble when an offensive man employs its use in a drive to the basket. The term dribble as we use it can only apply when we are trying to get the ball to the wings or pivot position.

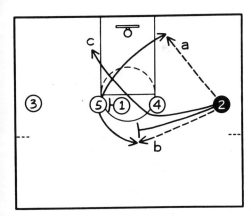

Figure 2-10

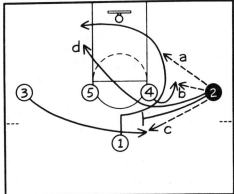

Figure 2-11

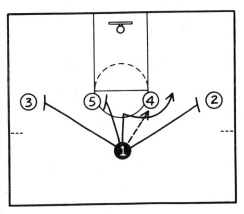

Figure 2-12

If the point man cannot get the ball to the pivot or wings by passing, he will dribble it to either one of the two positions. Thus the dribble in our 1-4 offense takes the place of a pass. The only reason he would not be able to get the ball to the pivot or wing positions with a pass would be defensive pressure. So one of the weapons we use to combat defensive pressure is the dribble, a free-lance move. We initiate the dribble into our offense so that it can be controlled and therefore become part of our controlled offense as well. Let's consider the dribble to the wing position first. To aid us in making this play a principal factor of our 1-4 offense, we must have our wing men adhere to Rule 3:

> RULE 3: Wing men must clear every time the point man dribbles the ball to the wing position.

In Figure 2-13, as point man 0-1 dribbles the ball toward 0-2, 0-2 must clear. 0-2 has four possible clearing maneuvers:

   a. Clear to the low post and go to the corner.
   b. Clear to the low post.
   c. Clear to the low post and go opposite.
   d. Clear to the low post and go to the point position.

In Figure 2-13, as 0-1 dribbles the ball toward 0-2, 0-1 can pass the ball to 0-4 whenever 0-4 is clear at the foul line or when cutting to the basket. If 0-1 cannot pass to 0-4, he should then look to pass off to 0-2 in position *a, b,* or *d.* If he passes the ball to 0-2 at *a,* 0-1 then has the same screening opportunities as 0-2 in Figure 2-5. If 0-1 passes the ball to 0-2 at *d,* 0-1 becomes a wing man and plays the wing position. 0-2 then becomes a point man and will play the point.

> RULE 4: On-side pivotmen must screen and roll for any dribbler or driver coming near them.

If the point man is being pressured by his defensive man, he can dribble toward a pivotman and get the pivotman to set a screen for him, as illustrated in Figure 2-14.

This concludes our discussion of the development of the 1-4 offense from a dribble.

The Development of the 1-4 Offense from a Drive

In the 1-4 offense the drive to the basket is constantly being sought. The drive to the basket takes precedence over any play pattern that has been entered into. Once a play pattern has been started, our players do not have to wait until it is completed before they are permitted to drive.

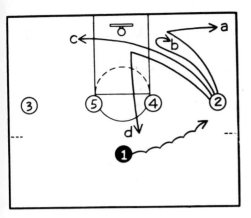

Figure 2-13

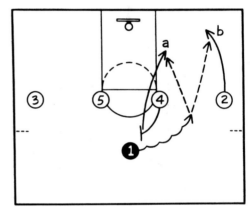

Figure 2-14

The offensive player with the ball is encouraged to take advantage of the drive opportunity without any hesitation just as soon as he becomes aware of its development. Consequently, all team members must constantly anticipate a possible drive to the basket from their teammate in possession of the ball at any time and from any place on the floor.

To initiate the discussion of the drive to the basket from various floor positions, let's begin by analyzing the possible drive outlets from the point position.

In Figure 2-15, the point man has three possible drive outlets:

a. A drive straight to the basket.
b. A drive to his right.
c. A drive to his left.

In order for point man 0-1 to drive straight to the basket as indicated by *a* in Figure 2-15, he must have created the opportunity by

35

maneuvering his defensive man completely out of position, or by having the defensive man nowhere near him to begin with. He can maneuver his defensive man out of position by using a cross-over dribble and dribbling straight up the middle, or by using a reverse dribble so successfully that he gets ahead of the defensive man and has a clear path to the basket.

In each case the pivotmen should treat the situation in the same manner as they would a fast-break opportunity. In Figure 2-16 both pivotmen 0-4 and 0-5 should break to the basket. 0-1 has the opportunity to drive all the way to the basket for a shot or to drop the ball off to either 0-4 or 0-5.

If point man 0-1 decides to take advantage of a drive opportunity to his right he must drive as close to 0-4 as possible. Because of Rule 4, 0-4 must set a screen for 0-1, then roll to the basket (Figure 2-17). This same rule would apply to 0-5 if 0-1 had driven to his left.

Wing men 0-3 and 0-2 can also drive to the basket whenever they are in possession of the ball. There are two drive opportunities available to them, the drive left and the drive right (Figure 2-18).

If 0-2 drives to his right, we ask our pivotmen to treat it in the same manner as they would if they were taking part in a side fast-break opportunity (Figure 2-19):

1. 0-2 drives right.
2. 0-4 pivots, faces the ball, and becomes the middle man in the fast break.
3. 0-5 breaks for the basket.

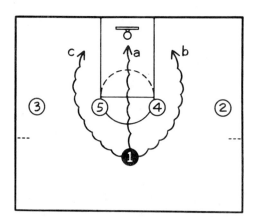

Figure 2-15

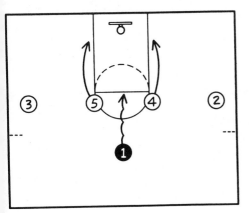

Figure 2-16

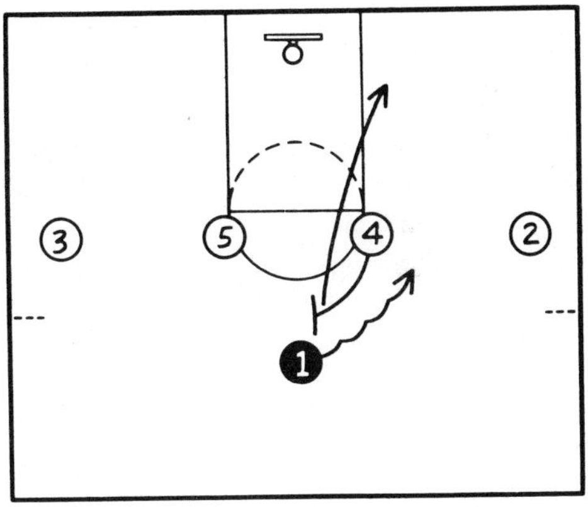

Figure 2-17

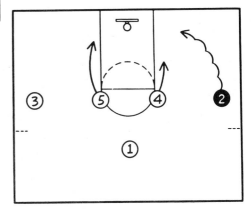

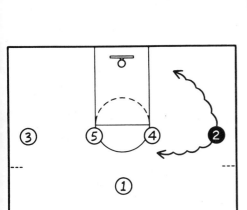

Figure 2-18

Figure 2-19

If 0-2 decides to drive to his left, he must drive as close to 0-4 as possible, trying to give 0-4 an opportunity to set a screen and roll to the basket (Figure 2-20).

1. 0-2 drives off 0-4.
2. 0-4 sets a screen for 0-2 and rolls to the basket.

Pivotmen 0-4 and 0-5 are asked to look for a drive opportunity every time they are in possession of the ball. They have the opportunity to drive to the basket as they are facing it or with their backs to it. In either case they have just two drive opportunities, a drive right and a drive left (Figure 2-21).

Development of the 1-4 Offense from a Shot

All basketball coaches realize the importance of good shooting. For any offense to be successful, good shooting is an absolute necessity.

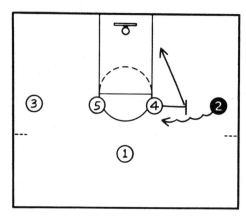

Figure 2-20

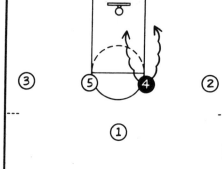

Figure 2-21

However, offensively most coaches believe that games are usually won from shots that have been missed, rebounded, and shot the second and third time. It is often said that the team that gets the second and third shot at the basket is the team that will win. Defensively we believe that if we can limit the opponent to one shot at the basket and rebound those shots that miss, we will win. Therefore, I believe that in the development of our 1-4 offense from a shot, two important factors must be considered:

1. Organized offensive rebounding once the shot is taken.
2. Organized defensive floor balance once the shot is taken.

Before we get into the actual organization of our offensive rebounding and defensive floor balance, I think it would be wise for us to explain our philosophy pertaining to these aspects of the game.

In our discussion of the point man, it was pointed out that he must be the complete basketball player. In most cases it is very unlikely that a boy with these qualities also has height. It is difficult to find a boy 6′ 2″ or 6′ 3″ who can be used as the point player. Most of us are forced to play a boy 5′ 9″ to 6′ 0″ at the point. When we do, however, we are faced with several problems. The small boy just can't be relied upon to rebound under the boards time and time again. He can be asked to rebound against a bigger boy maybe once or twice during the course of the game, but constant rebounding against him takes too much out of the small man and will have a tremendous effect on his over-all game efficiency. To protect the small point man, we give no rebounding responsibilities under the boards. Instead, after every shot he is asked to rebound around the foul line area. In this position he has a good opportunity to pick off long rebounds or those that have deflected toward him.

In regard to defensive floor balance, the small point player confronts us with another problem. Picture in your mind for a moment the ordeal facing the small point man defending against a two-on-one situation where the two men coming down with the ball are 6′2″ or better. Picture him defending against the three-on-one fast-break with a similar or even greater height disadvantage. In both cases he is courting disaster. He may be able to cope with such situations occasionally, but he cannot be relied upon to do the job as consistently as a bigger boy could. To protect the small point man from such situations, our point man never has the responsibility of becoming the first man back unless he has thrown a bad pass and an interception has taken place. Instead he is given the responsibility of being the second man back on defense, thus never having to defend under the basket against big driving forwards or centers.

With these thoughts expressed for your understanding of the adjustments we make to protect the small point player, we can now present our rebounding and defensive floor balance procedures:

RULE 5: The off-side pivotman sinks to and rebounds the off side.

RULE 6: The on-side wing man has middle rebounding responsibilities on all shots.

RULE 7: The off-side wing man must be the first man down court to protect against a possible fast break.

Figure 2-22 illustrates offensive rebounding and defensive floor balance procedures after a shot is taken by point man 0-1 from the right side of the top of the key. Here 0-2, prior to 0-1's shot, moves towards the corner. After 0-1 shoots the ball, 0-2 has the middle rebounding position, 0-5 rebounds the off side, 0-4 rebounds the strong side, and 0-1 rebounds near the foul line more or less as a half rebounder. Wing man 0-3, since the shot is taken from his off side, must move out so he can be in good position to be the first man down court to protect defensively against a possible fast break.

Figure 2-23 illustrates offensive rebounding and defensive floor balance procedures after a shot is taken by wing man 0-2. Here, after wing man 0-2 shoots the ball, 0-4 rebounds the strong side, 0-5 rebounds the weak side, 0-1 follows his rule and becomes a half rebounder near the foul area, 0-2 follows his shot, and wing man 0-3 must move out to a position where he can become the first man down court to protect defensively against the fast break.

Figure 2-24 illustrates offensive rebounding and defensive floor balance procedures after a shot is taken by pivotman 0-4. Here, after 0-4 shoots the ball, 0-4 follows his shot, 0-2 rebounds the strong side, 0-5 rebounds the weak-side, point man 0-1 becomes a half rebounder near the foul area, and wing man 0-3 moves out and protects against a possible fast break.

Figure 2-25 illustrates offensive rebounding and defensive floor

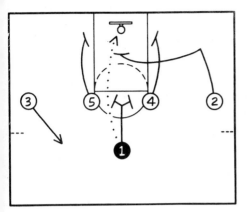

Figure 2-22

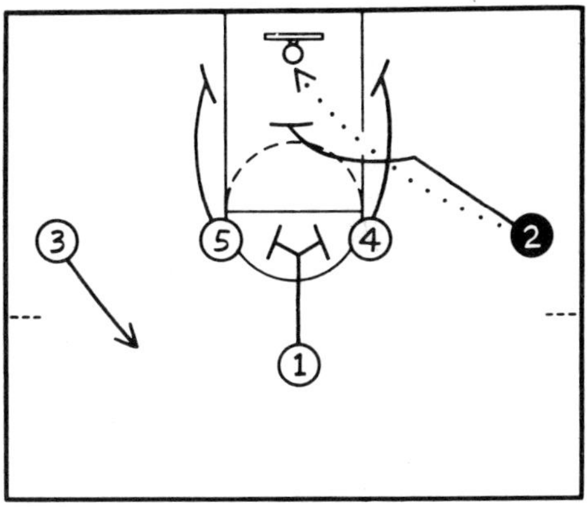

Figure 2-23

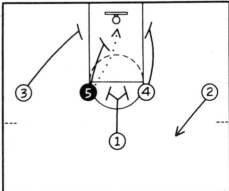

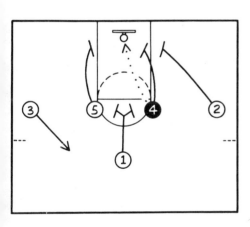

Figure 2-24

Figure 2-25

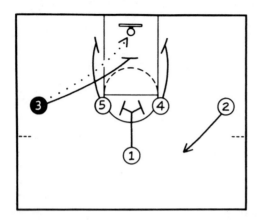

Figure 2-26

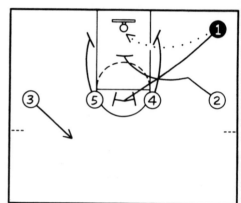

Figure 2-27

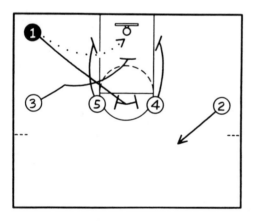

Figure 2-28

balance procedures after a shot is taken by pivotman 0-5. Here, after 0-5 shoots the ball, 0-5 follows his shot, wing man 0-3 rebounds the strong side, 0-4 rebounds the weak side, 0-1 becomes a half rebounder near the foul area, and wing man 0-2 moves out to protect defensively against the fast break.

Figure 2-26 illustrates the offensive rebounding and defensive floor balance procedures after a shot is taken by wing man 0-3. Here after 0-3 shoots the ball, 0-3 follows his shot, 0-5 rebounds the strong side, 0-4 rebounds the weak side, 0-1 becomes a half rebounder near the foul area, and 0-2 protects defensively against the fast break.

Figure 2-27 illustrates the offensive rebounding and the defensive floor balance procedures after a shot is taken by point man 0-1 from the right corner. Here, after 0-1 takes a shot from the corner, 0-1 follows his shot, 0-2 has middle rebounding responsibilities, 0-4 rebounds the strong side, 0-5 rebounds the weak side, and 0-3 moves out to protect defensively.

Figure 2-28 illustrates the offensive rebounding and the defensive floor balance procedures after a shot is taken by point man 0-1 from the left corner. Here, after 0-1 shoots the ball, 0-1 follows his shot, 0-3 has middle rebounding responsibility, 0-5 becomes the strong side rebounder, 0-4 rebounds the weak side, and 0-2 protects defensively against the fast break.

This concludes our discussion of the development of the 1-4 offense from plays initiated by a pass, dribble, shot, or drive, and we're now ready to develop the specific plays used in our 1-4 offense.

3

PLAY 1: PASS AND CUT,

CLEAR TO THE OPPOSITE SIDE

The old pass and cut has been the most successful play ever to be evolved from the game of basketball. It can be used as an offense in itself by having the players cut to the basket after each time they pass the ball. It can be worked over and over again, and eventually the shot will be created. At one time just prior to the advent of pressure defenses, the popularity of the pass and cut was probably at its lowest ebb. Those were the days when controlled offenses such as the shuffle, wheel, swing-and-go and others were used successfully by many coaches. As the pressure defenses became more persistent, the popularity of those controlled offenses decreased somewhat. As their use decreased, a resurgence in the popularity of the pass and cut developed. The thought behind the use of the pass and cut to combat pressure defenses is that its use quickly frees the offensive man who is being guarded closely, and if successful the good close-in percentage shot develops. Although the pass and cut can be used successfully against pressure defenses, we use it as part of our offense for a number of other good reasons, the two most important being:

1. It creates a space that the man with the ball can penetrate to with the least amount of harassment.
2. It sets up a number of opportunities to develop a good off-side play which, I believe, is the most important single ingredient leading to any type of successful offense.

Let's develop the *Pass and Cut, Clear to the Opposite Side* and all its options and see how they adhere to the conditions stated above.

One of the major obstacles facing the point man in our 1-4 offense is getting the ball in play to the wing men. Previously we stated that we like our point man to dribble down court and penetrate to the head of the key. In our offense, a pass to the wing man from the head of the key is a very dangerous maneuver. The chance of completing such a pass without an interception by a defensive man is very unlikely. The vulnerability of such a pass is due to the relatively long distances between the point man and the wing man. In Figure 3-1, the distances between the point man and the wing man in the 1-4 offense are illustrated. Compare such distances with Figure 3-2, which illustrates the distances between a guard and a forward in a 2-3 offense.

To overcome the greater distance between the point man and the wing man in the 1-4 offense, we ask the point man, after he penetrates to the head of the key, to shorten this distance by taking a few dribbles toward the wing man. We like him to move from the head of the key to a position comparable to that one occupied by 0-2 in Figure 3-2.

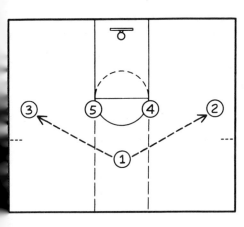

Figure 3-1

Figure 3-2

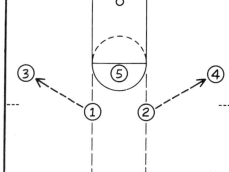

He is taught to move to this position by taking his left foot and placing it across the right one, putting the point man in a position where his back is turned on his defensive man.

As the left foot is placed in such a position, we ask him to dribble hard with his right hand. He dribbles the ball, taking short shuffling steps until he has reached his desired position. In doing so he must make sure that the left foot is always the lead foot and the right one never advances in front of the left.

This action also serves as a key, indicating to the wing man that the point man wants to pass him the ball. Therefore, every time the point man dribbling the ball shuffles toward the wing man, the latter must get himself clear of his defender so that he can receive a pass from the point man. This action of a wing man freeing himself to receive a pass from a point man has on many occasions been the subject of great debate. Many coaches believe that it is advantageous to have the wing man free himself in a particular way. Some go so far as to ask the wing man to receive the pass from the point man with a certain foot in advance of the other. We believe this suggestion has merit; however, we don't spend much time trying to train our own wing men to receive a pass with a certain foot leading, because under game conditions we have found our players, upon receiving the ball, paying little attention to which foot is forward.

We believe that if a wing man is closely guarded and knows he must free himself from a defender in order to receive a pass, he can do so with the freedom of his own movements much more easily than with anything we can give him. The only thing we tell our wing men that helps set them free is to take their defensive man in toward the basket, then break out to the wing position as quickly as possible. The penetration toward the basket from the wing man should be in a straight line. If the wing man penetrates in this manner, the defensive man must go inside with him. The one thing we caution our wing men not to do is penetrate to the basket in an arc that carries them toward the corner. If they penetrate in this manner, the defensive man has a definite advantage. It is much easier for a defensive man to keep the wing man from receiving a pass when he arcs than when he darts in straight lines.

Pass and Cut Option 1: Hit the Cutter

In Figure 3-3 point man 0-1 executes the key for putting the ball in play to 0-2. 0-2 penetrates toward the basket and quickly darts back to his wing position to receive a pass from 0-1, who, after initiating the key, continues his dribble until he is ready to pass the ball to 0-2. We want our point man to pass off the dribble to 0-2 rather than have him pick up the ball before 0-2 has made his proper moves. After 0-2 makes his moves, 0-1 passes the ball to him, making sure that the pass is thrown away from the defensive man and to the outside of 0-2.

After point man 0-1 passes the ball to 0-2, he steps toward 0-5. Starting with the right foot, 0-1 should take two steps toward 0-5. Once the second step is taken with the left foot, 0-1 plants that foot, changes direction, and cuts to the outside of 0-4. As 0-1 cuts off 0-4 he should try to be close enough to him so that his defensive man either bumps into 0-4, goes behind 0-4, or follows 0-1 to the basket.

As 0-1 is maneuvering himself into position to execute his cut to the basket, 0-2 after receiving the ball turns and faces his defensive man. Facing his defensive man puts him in good position to see 0-1 cutting to the basket and to decide to pass him the ball. If 0-1's defensive man runs into 0-4 or follows 0-1 to the basket, 0-1 should attempt to shoot a lay-up shot, provided:

1. 0-4's defensive man did not switch off to pick up 0-1.
2. 0-5's defensive man sagging leaves 0-5 and gives the required weak-side support necessary to shut off 0-1's lay-up.

If 0-5's defensive man has switched off and picked up 0-1 cutting, 0-1 can possibly try the power move, but if the defensive man has too great a height advantage and good defensive position, 0-1 should not attempt the shot. Instead, he should stop, dribble away from the

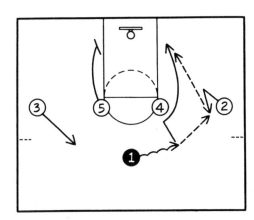

Figure 3-3

basket, and look for a possible pass to 0-4. 0-4 may be clear, or guarded by 0-1's defensive man. 0-1's defensive man guarding 0-4 close to the basket is a mismatch and 0-1 should get the ball to 0-4 as soon as possible. If 0-5's defensive man picks up 0-1 driving, 0-1 could possibly try a lay-up or power move. If 0-1 realizes what has occurred he should drop the ball off to 0-5 for a lay-up. 0-1, after receiving the ball from 0-2, must be aware of the possible defensive support that he will encounter. He must be made to understand fully that this support defense can be used to his team's advantage if he can make the appropriate counter-action.

Pass and Cut Option 2: Drive Off the Pivot

Figures 3-4 and 3-5 illustrate the drive off the pivot.

In Figure 3-4, after 0-1 passes 0-2 the ball he cuts off 0-4 toward the basket. Once 0-1 realizes he will not get a return pass from 0-2 he clears to the baseline on the opposite side of the floor. 0-2, upon receiving the ball, faces his defensive man. Once he decides not to pass the ball to 0-1 cutting, he must then execute a power thrust with his right foot toward the baseline. If he feels he can drive toward the basket, he may do so. However, if he decides not to drive, the power thrust movement toward the baseline will set up his defensive man so that he can be screened off easily by 0-4. In Figure 3-4, on a pass to wing man 0-2, 0-4 has three possible options. They are:

1. Screen toward the ball for 0-2.
2. Screen away from the ball for 0-5.
3. Cut to the basket.

Pivotman 0-4 Screens Toward the Ball

If 0-4 decides to screen toward the ball for 0-2 (Figure 3-5), 0-2 must wait until 0-4 takes a stationary position next to 0-2's defensive man. The position taken by 0-4 next to 0-2's defensive man should be one in which:

1. He is as close to the defensive man as is legally possible.
2. His feet are somewhere near shoulder width.
3. His inside hand, his left in this case, is carried on his left hip.
4. He stands erect, positioning his body so that his head is in front of the defensive man's body rather than behind it.

Once 0-4 has set the screen on 0-2's defensive man, 0-2 makes a cross-over move and executes a drive left. In his drive left all of the rules governing the one-on-one moves go into effect. If he can drive all the way or shoot the jump shot he is free to do so.

Once 0-2 starts his drive, 0-4 rolls to the basket. If 0-4's defensive man picks up 0-2, 0-2 must get the ball back to 0-4 as soon as pos-

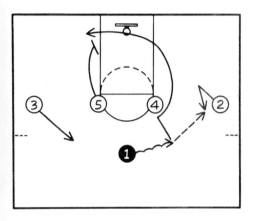

Figure 3-4

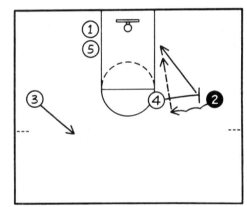

Figure 3-5

sible, completing the screen and roll play (Figure 3-5). If 0-2 cannot pass the ball to 0-4 rolling to the basket, and cannot shoot or drive to the basket himself, his next responsibility is to put the ball in play on the off side of the court. He enters into what we call our weak-side series (Figure 3-6). Here, pivotman 0-4 sets an inside screen for wing man 0-2, then rolls to the basket. After the screen, wing man 0-2 drives for the foul line. If 0-2's actions indicate he is not going to

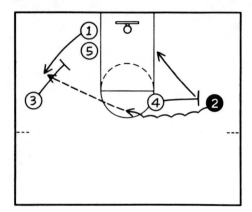

Figure 3-6

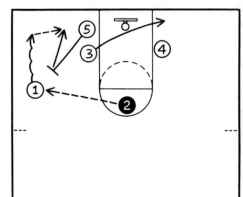

Figure 3-7

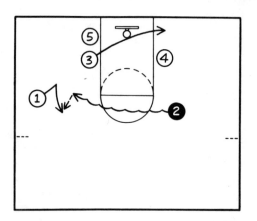

Figure 3-8

shoot or pass to 0-4, 0-3 screens down for 0-1. Point man 0-1 moves out to receive the pass from 0-2, then looks for a shot.

Our weak-side series is initiated by wing man 0-3 after he is positive the on-side options available to 0-2 have been defensed successfully and can't be developed into a percentage shot. Wing man 0-3's first move is to screen down for point man 0-1 who is waiting near the baseline for the weak-side series to begin. We ask 0-3 to take a starting position as close to 0-5 as possible. He should have his right foot placed as close as possible to 0-5's right foot. Once he assumes this position, it's 0-1's responsibility to run his defensive man into 0-3. An effective screen can be assured by having 0-3 force 0-1's defensive man to follow a path to the outside of 0-3's left arm. If the screen is effective, 0-2 passes 0-1 the ball. If 0-1 has a shot, he shoots the ball. If, however, 0-1 is able to receive the pass from 0-2, but is unable to take a shot, then 0-5 has a responsibility to become part of the play. We ask 0-5 to set a baseline screen for 0-1 (Figure 3-7), in which play 0-2 passes the ball to 0-1, and 0-5 sets a baseline screen for 0-1, then rolls to the basket. Point man 0-1 passes to 0-5 rolling or takes the shot if it develops. If a shot is taken, wing man 0-3 has middle rebounding responsibilities. If not he clears around 0-4. Pivotman 0-4 rebounds the off side and wing man 0-2 protects defensively against the fast break.

The success of the weak-side series depends upon a good screen by 0-3 to clear 0-1 momentarily so that 0-1 can receive a pass from 0-2. Many times this pass from 0-2 to 0-1, for a number of reasons, cannot be made. Some of the more frequently recurring reasons are poor screening by 0-3, a switch on defense performed between 0-1's defensive man and that of 0-3's, and simply an absolute oversight by 0-2. If any one of these situations arises, stopping the pass to 0-1, 0-2 must continue dribbling across the foul area and carry the ball to 0-1, handing it off as they interchange (Figure 3-8).

In this case, if 0-1 can shoot the ball after receiving the pass, he does. If he cannot shoot the ball, he looks for a drive to the basket. If a drive to the basket is not available, he will dribble the ball across the foul area over to the pivotman 0-4's side of the court. Once 0-3 becomes aware of 0-1's dribble, using 0-4 as a screen, 0-3 breaks up from the baseline to receive a pass from 0-1. 0-3, after receiving the pass, has the same opportunities available to him as 0-1 in Figure 3-7. If 0-1 cannot pass the ball to 0-3, 0-1 will continue dribbling and carry the ball to 0-3, handing it off as they interchange. 0-3 can shoot or drive, carrying the ball over to 0-2 for a possible interchange, or pass the ball to 0-2 for a possible screen and roll play between 0-2 and 0-5. We will continue this continuity from one side of the floor to the other until a shot develops.

Many ball clubs force us to use our weak-side series as an automatic. We go to our weak-side series automatically whenever our point man's defensive man refuses to follow him all the way to the off side.

Most good defensive clubs will hold up a man in the low post to take away the screen and roll play instead of clearing him to the off side along with his offensive man. When such defensive tactics are employed, our offensive man in possession of the ball will immediately take the ball to the off side and enter into our weak-side series.

In Figure 3-5, pivotman 0-4 elected to set a screen toward the ball for wing man 0-2. He could have elected to screen away from the ball for pivotman 0-5, as illustrated in Figure 3-9.

Here 0-5 can follow Route A to a low post position or Route B to a high post position. If 0-2 does not pass the ball to 0-5, no matter what route 0-5 has taken he must become part of the play by screening for 0-2.

If 0-5 follows Route B he sets the inside screen in the same manner as was outlined previously for 0-4 in Figure 3-5. If 0-5 follows Route A and does not get the ball from 0-2, 0-5 moves out of the low post position and becomes part of the play by setting a baseline screen for 0-2 (Figure 3-10).

Once 0-5 sets the screen for 0-2, 0-2 fakes to his inside and executes a drive right. 0-2 can shoot a jump shot or drive to the basket. If 0-5's defensive man picks up 0-2 driving, 0-5 rolls to the basket and receives a pass from 0-2.

If pivotman 0-4 screens for 0-5 and 0-5 follows Route A (Figure 3-9), 0-2 should make the pass into him. If 0-5 is clear he shoots the ball. If 0-5 receives the ball with a man on him, 0-5 is still close enough to the basket to enter into a power move with his back to the basket. At any rate, if 0-5 gets the ball that close to the basket, a shot should develop.

If 0-5 follows Route B and is momentarily free enough to receive a pass from 0-2, 0-5 has the following options:

1. He can turn and shoot the jump shot.
2. He can drive, dribbling to the basket.

3. After receiving the ball he can turn and face his defensive man, then go one-on-one against him.
4. He can play with the man who has passed him the ball.

If 0-5 decides to play with 0-2, the man who has passed him the ball, he must realize that 0-2 has these options available to him:

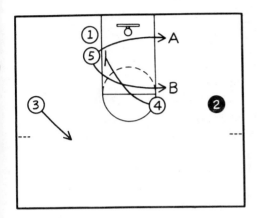

Figure 3-9

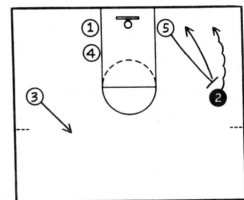

Figure 3-10

1. Option 3, pass to the pivot and go behind.
2. Option 4, pass to the pivot and screen.
3. Option 5, pass to the pivot and cut backdoor.

Figure 3-11 illustrates Option 3, pass to the pivot and go behind. Here the wing man 0-2 passes the ball to 0-5 and cuts towards 0-5's defensive man. As he approaches him, 0-2 changes the direction of his cut and drops behind 0-5. 0-5 drops the ball off to 0-2, then cuts to the basket. 0-2 can shoot the ball or return it to 0-5 rolling to the basket. 0-3 on the pass to 0-5 screens down for 0-1. 0-1 moves out to 0-3's position for defensive balance. 0-4 rebounds the weak side.

If in Figure 3-11, 0-2 cannot pass the ball to 0-5 or shoot the ball himself, he must look for 0-1 and enter into one weak-side series. The weak-side series remains in operation until a shot can be taken.

Figure 3-12 illustrates Option 4, pass to the pivot and screen. Here wing man 0-2 passes the ball to 0-5 and sets an inside screen. 0-5 dribbles off the screen; 0-2 rolls to the basket. 0-5 passes to 0-2; 0-4 rebounds the strong side. 0-1 becomes a half rebounder at the foul area; 0-3 moves out for defensive balance.

In Figure 3-12, 0-5 after receiving the ball from 0-2 also has the option of shooting the ball off the screen or driving to the basket.

Figure 3-13 illustrates Option 5, pass to the pivot and cut backdoor. Here wing man 0-2 passes the ball to pivotman 0-5, steps toward 0-5, and then cuts to the basket. Pivotman 0-5 passes the ball to 0-2 for a shot. Pivotman 0-4 rebounds the off side. Point man 0-1 moves to the foul area to rebound. Wing man 0-3 moves out for defensive balance.

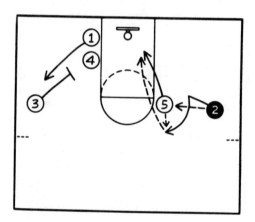

Figure 3-11

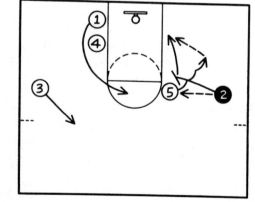

Figure 3-12

Many times in the situation shown in Figure 3-13, 0-5 cannot pass the ball to 0-2. If the pass cannot be made, 0-5 can shoot the ball, wait until 0-2 clears to the opposite side of the court and go one-on-one against his defensive man, or enter into the weak-side series. If 0-5 decides to enter into the weak-side series he must key the play by dribbling the ball toward the off side. Once he dribbles, 0-3 screens down for point man 0-1 and the weak-side series is set in motion.

This exhausts all the options of Play 1, *Pass and Cut, Clear to the Opposite Side.* We are now ready to have our point man pass the ball to the wing man, cut toward the basket, and go to the corner.

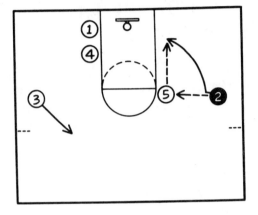

Figure 3-13

4

PLAY 2: PASS AND CUT,

GO TO THE CORNER

The point man, after passing the ball, must move to a new floor position. In the *Pass and Cut, Clear to the Opposite Side,* the point man took his defensive man to the side of the floor away from the ball. In the *Pass and Cut, Go to the Corner,* the point man, after passing the ball to a wing man, cuts to the basket and goes to the corner on the same side of the floor as the ball (Figure 4-1).

On any pass from a point man to a wing man, the on-side pivotman, 0-4, must decide on one of three courses of action. He has his choice of cutting to the basket, screening away from the ball for pivotman 0-5, or screening toward the ball for wing man 0-2.

A cut to the basket by 0-4 usually takes place after 0-4 has set a screen a few times for wing man 0-2. 0-4's defensive man begins to anticipate this screen for 0-2 and fails to make the necessary adjustments to protect the pivotman cutting to the basket. Let's stop for a moment and analyze defensive adjustments that must be made by 0-4's defensive man on a pass to wing man 0-2.

Figure 4-2 illustrates the defensing of a pivotman when the ball is at the point position. X-4 must play to the inside of 0-4 whenever 0-1 has the ball. If 0-1 passes the ball to 0-2, defensive man X-4 must make an adjustment. X-4 must go to the baseline side of 0-4 just as quickly as possible. The manner in which X-4 should make this adjustment is of little concern to us. It matters little if X-4 goes behind 0-4 to get to his baseline side (Figure 4-3), or if X-4 goes over the

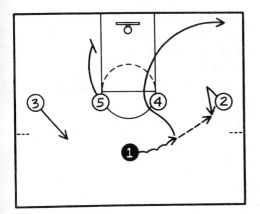

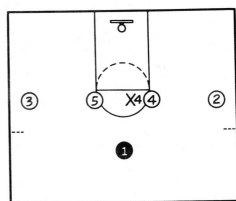

Figure 4-1

Figure 4-2

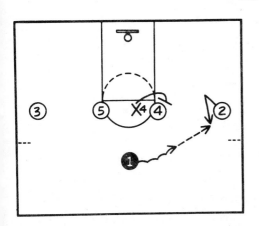

Figure 4-3

top of 0-4 to reach the same position (Figure 4-4). The point is that X-4 must make this adjustment.

If X-4 fails to make this adjustment any time the ball is passed to 0-2, 0-4 must cut to the basket. In such situations no other plays are necessary. If given such an opportunity, we will pass the ball to 0-4 time and time again until X-4 adjusts properly.

In Figure 4-5, the key for such a play rests in the hands of the pivot-

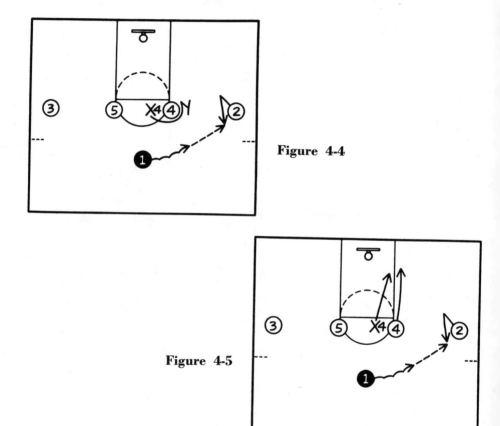

Figure 4-4

Figure 4-5

man. Just as soon as the ball is passed to the wing position, the offensive pivot should become aware of his defensive man's position. If he fails to make the necessary adjustment, the offensive pivotman breaks to the basket. I must admit that these defensive flaws seldom occur on the first pass, but in the event they do our pivotman is equipped to take advantage of them.

If, on a pass to the wing man 0-2, 0-4 cuts to the basket and doesn't receive the ball, he must clear to the opposite side (Figure 4-6). Pivot-man 0-5 must move to the strong side and become part of the play.

In this play, as well as in the rest of our offense, 0-5 must always be aware of 0-4's actions. The success of the 1-4 offense is largely depend-ent upon how well 0-4 and 0-5 work together. With the pivotman given so much freedom in the execution of our plays in order to main-

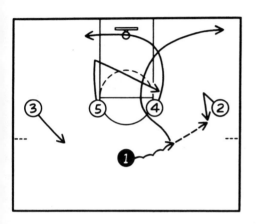

Figure 4-6

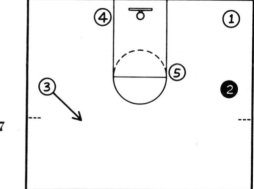

Figure 4-7

tain proper floor balance at all times, it is imperative that the pivotmen keep an eye on each other.

The options that are developed from our pass and cut, go to the corner will unfold from an overload alignment on the strong side of the court (Figure 4-7).

In this alignment, 0-2, as a result of 0-1's moving into the corner, has his movement with the ball confined to a drive left. 0-1's presence in the corner prevents him from driving to his right, making the drive left his only avenue of pursuit. With 0-1 in the corner, the screen and roll between 0-4 and 0-2 is a marginal play. Its success is rather limited and depends upon how much support 0-1's defensive man can give. We do not recommend the use of such a play from this particular setup.

Since the screen and roll play from this alignment is a marginal one, we don't incorporate its use into our overall offense. To make absolutely sure that 0-4 does not come over to screen for 0-2, every time the point man goes to the corner, we make 0-4 cut to the basket and clear to the opposite side or screen away for 0-5. Usually before the point man goes to the corner, 0-4 is given one of the two following keys:

1. Before point man 0-1 cuts through he yells "Corner."
2. Point man 0-1, on his way to the corner, will cut to the inside of 0-4, instead of to his outside (Figure 4-6).

From here to the end of the chapter, it will be taken for granted that 0-4 has cut to the basket or has screened away from the ball for 0-5. If 0-4's defensive man is in the proper baseline side position, 0-4 pivots on his right foot, turns his back on the ball, and screens down for 0-5. If 0-4's defensive man is to set up to the right of 0-4, 0-4 will cut to the basket, and if he does not receive a pass from 0-2, he will clear to the opposite side.

In reviewing our discussion up to this point, you may have been led to believe that 0-1's presence in the corner is more a detriment than an asset. It is definitely a detriment to 0-2. This alignment is not designed to set up 0-2 as a shooter; in this alignment 0-2 is used primarily as a passer, screener, and cutter. Even though he does have the option of driving off the pivot for a shot, most of the plays from this setup will not involve 0-2 as the primary shooter. With these thoughts in mind and serving as background material, I believe we can now enter the six options of Play 2: *Pass and Cut, Go to the Corner.*

Option 1: Drive Off the Pivot

In Figure 4-8, point man 0-1 has passed the ball and has already gone to the corner; wing man 0-2 executes a drive left, driving close enough to 0-5 so as to try to rub his man off. After 0-2 dribbles by, 0-5 rolls to the basket and 0-2 can shoot the ball or pass to 0-5 rolling. 0-1 moves out to get to his rebounding position. Pivotman 0-4 sinks to and rebounds the off side. Wing man 0-3 takes two steps out and protects against the fast break. If 0-2 drives close enough to 0-5, 0-2 will get a shot provided:

1. 0-5's defensive man does not switch to pick him up.
2. 0-3's defensive man does not sag off 0-3 to stop the shot.

If 0-4's defensive man switches off to pick up 0-2 driving, 0-2 should try to get the ball back to 0-5 rolling to the basket. If he is unable to hit 0-5 rolling, then he must enter into our weak-side series.

The weak-side series from such a drive by 0-2 is not as effective as the weak-side series presented earlier in Chapter 3. Here we are working with just two people on the off side, 0-3 and 0-4, whereas in the *Pass and Cut, Clear to the Opposite Side* we had three people.

Since the alignment is not designed primarily for 0-2 to be a shooter, if he attempts to find a shooting opportunity he places us in a somewhat weakened position on the weak side. Nevertheless we encourage 0-2 to take advantage of the drive left. If he does so and a shot is not forthcoming, he must get the ball to 0-3.

The three ways in which 0-2 can get the ball to 0-3 are:

1. Pass the ball directly to him.
2. Carry the ball to him by means of the dribble.
3. Hand the ball off to him as 0-3 cuts behind him.

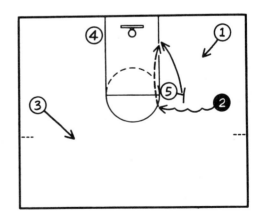

Figure 4-8

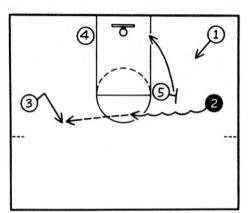

Figure 4-9

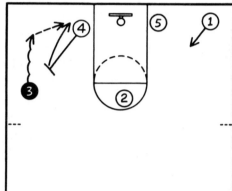

Figure 4-10

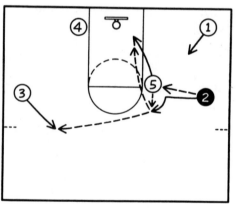

Figure 4-11

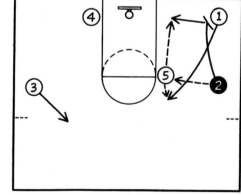

Figure 4-12

The success of a pass depends largely on 0-3's freeing himself by faking down toward the basket and darting back out (Figure 4-9).

In Figure 4-10, with 0-3 having the ball, 0-4 enters into the play by setting a baseline screen for 0-3. As 0-3 drives toward the baseline, 0-4 rolls to the basket, and 0-3 can shoot the ball or hit 0-4 rolling to the basket.

If in Figure 4-9, 0-2 cannot pass the ball to 0-3, then 0-2 must dribble it over to him and hand it off as they interchange. 0-3 can shoot the ball, start a new play, or continue the interchange by dribbling the ball over to 0-1. Earlier we made the statement that in the alignment shown in Figure 4-7 the major functions of 0-2 were to act as a passer, screener, or cutter. If we consider 0-2 as a passer, we find that he can pass the ball to 0-5 in the pivot, to 0-1 in the corner, or if necessary, to 0-3 who must come over to help out. Let us first consider the pass to the pivot and the options it makes available.

Option 2: Pass to the Pivot and Go Behind

In Figure 4-11, after 0-2 passes to 0-5, 0-2 cuts behind 0-5 and receives a return pass. If 0-2 cannot shoot the ball or pass to 0-5 rolling, then 0-2 looks for 0-3 to set up the off-side series. If 0-2 passes to 0-3, then 0-4 will set a baseline screen for 0-2. If 0-2 has to hand the ball off to 0-3, then 0-3 shoots the ball or sets up the interchange series.

Option 3: Pass to the Pivot and Screen Down
for the Point Man

The pass to the pivot and go behind can be used successfully if 0-5 receives the ball at the high post. However, when 0-4 screens for 0-5, 0-5 usually receives the ball from 0-2 in the low or medium post positions. 0-2 should give 0-5 an opportunity to shoot the ball, or the time necessary to determine the possibility of a shot.

If 0-2 passes the ball to 0-5 in the low post position, 0-5 should shoot the ball immediately or shoot after going one-on-one with his defensive man. If 0-5 receives the ball from 0-2 in the medium post position, 0-2 should give 0-5 an opportunity to look for a shot. To give 0-5 time to decide, 0-2 screens down in the corner for 0-1 (Figure 4-12).

If in Figure 4-12, 0-5 cannot hand the ball off to 0-1 or 0-2, he looks for 0-3 on the off side. A pass to 0-3 from the position of 0-5 could be very dangerous, especially if 0-3 has a defensive man close to him.

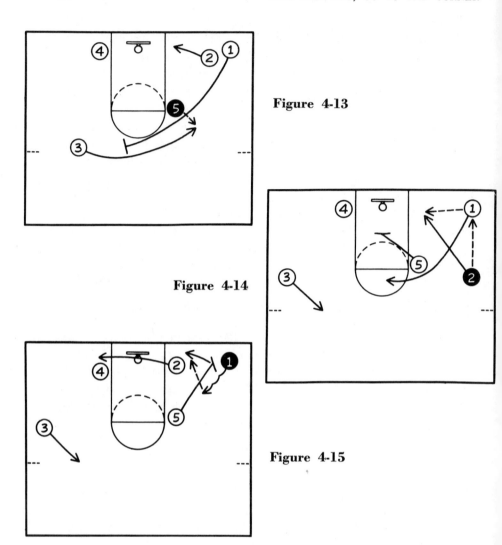

Figure 4-13

Figure 4-14

Figure 4-15

If 0-5 gets stuck with the ball, we give 0-3 the responsibility of getting clear so that he can gain possession of the ball from 0-5. The best way for him to get clear is to cut off 0-1, using 0-1 as a screener (Figure 4-13).

Option 4: Pass to the Corner and Clear to the Opposite Side

The pass to the corner and clear to the opposite side is our most productive play in the corner series. Options 1, 2, and 3 are plays that come about mostly through defensive errors. In our offense we must make our players aware of these three options, but the play we're really looking for is the forward clearing to the opposite side. This play gives us several strongside options and at the same time sets up our weak-side series in the desired manner.

The strongside series includes:

1. A pass and cut option.
2. A screen and roll option.

Figure 4-14 illustrates the pass and cut between the wing man and the corner man. Here 0-2 passes to 0-1, 0-2 cuts for the basket, 0-1 passes the ball to 0-2 cutting, 0-5 rebounds the middle rebounding position, 0-1 moves out to the foul area, and 0-4 rebounds the weak side.

In Figure 4-14, if 0-2's defensive man is between him and the ball when 0-2 cuts to the basket, it becomes impossible for 0-1 to return the ball to him. If 0-1 cannot return the ball to 0-2, then he must look to 0-5 to become part of the play by initiating the screen and roll option (Figure 4-15).

Here 0-2, after passing to 0-1, cuts and clears to the opposite side. 0-5 becomes a part of the play by screening for 0-1, then rolling to the basket. 0-1 puts the ball on the floor with a dribble and either shoots the ball or passes it to 0-5 rolling. 0-4 rebounds the weak side. 0-3 takes two steps out for defensive balance to protect against the fast break. If 0-1 cannot shoot the ball or pass it to 0-5 he must enter into our weak-side series, which has already been explained in Chapter 3.

Option 5: Pass to the Corner and Screen for the Point

After 0-2 passes the ball to point man 0-1 in the corner, he has three screening routes that he can follow (Figure 4-16):

1. He can follow the ball and screen for point man 0-1 in the corner.
2. He can pass the ball to 0-1 and screen for pivotman 0-5.
3. He can pass the ball to 0-1 and screen for the point.

Screening routes 1 and 2 above have already been discussed. Screening route 3 is another one of those options that we would rather have 0-2 stay away from. Whenever 0-2 screens for 0-3, the results are usually not too fruitful. Such a screen seems to bring about congestion more than it does a good shooting opportunity. It must be remem-

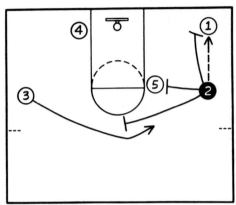

Figure 4-16

Figure 4-17

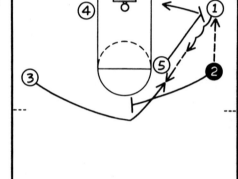

bered, however, that in our offense, wing man 0-2, after passing to the corner, is free to move in any direction. Therefore, to impress upon our players that it is impossible for them to make a mistake just as long as they move after passing the ball, I believe it is necessary to present this option of passing to the corner and screening for the point. Even though we shy away from the play, to be fair we should point out that it can be an excellent maneuver against teams that defensively fail to follow cutters through to the opposite sides.

Teams with such defensive techniques are very effective in defending against the screen or roll from the corner. Therefore, if 0-2 after passing to 0-1 in the corner screens at the point, his defensive man could not possibly defend against the screen and roll play that is being set up in Figure 4-17.

In this play wing man 0-2 passes the ball to point man 0-1 and screens away from the ball at the point. Pivotman 0-5 must become part of the play so he goes over to the corner and sets a screen for 0-1. 0-5 then rolls to the basket. Point man 0-1 dribbles off the screen. He can pass the ball to 0-5 rolling, shoot, or hand the ball off to 0-3 who has had a screen set for him by 0-2. 0-4 rebounds the off side.

Option 6: Pass Out to the Point and Shuffle

Option 6 employs the use of the ever popular shuffle cut. We incorporate the shuffle cut into our offense because: *(1) it gives us a set play we can call upon in tight situations; (2) it gives us something to go into whenever the defense forces us to pass the ball out to the point position; (3) it forces our opponents to use up valuable practice time preparing a defense to defend against its use.*

In our 1-4 offense we encourage the use of many free-lance movements. However, at certain times during the course of a ball game, strategy may call for the use of a set play. It may be after a time out, or it may be because we want to work for the lay-up shot, or we may want to maintain ball control. There are a number of situations in which a set play can be utilized. The point we want to make is that we feel every good offense should consist of several set plays that can be called upon at the discretion of the coach. The set play decided upon doesn't necessarily have to be the shuffle. It can be almost any play that has gained your confidence. We happen to use the shuffle because it gives us a little more weak-side offense to go with. In keeping with our rule of movement after passing the ball, the shuffle blends well where we're forced to throw the ball out from the wing position to the point.

The discussion that follows employs the use of the shuffle as a secondary pattern of play. In our discussion we're trying to set up the corner play, which, with its option, is considered our primary play.

If 0-2 upon receiving the ball cannot pass to 0-1 in the corner or 0-5 in the pivot and his defensive man is applying heavy pressure, he looks to pass the ball out to 0-3, thus keying the shuffle play (Figure 4-18).

In this situation, 0-3, seeing that 0-2 is having difficulty getting rid of the ball, moves in toward the basket, then angles out to receive the ball from 0-2. 0-2, because he is unable to throw the ball to 0-1 in the corner or to 0-5 in the pivot, looks for safety valve 0-3. Once 0-3 is clear, 0-2 passes him the ball. 0-1 moves in towards the basket; 0-5, after the pass to 0-3, steps up and sets a screen for 0-2; 0-4 breaks up from his rebounding position to a floor position where he can easily receive a pass from 0-3. 0-3 passes 0-4 the ball.

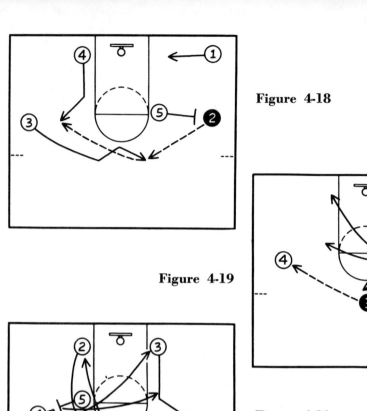

Figure 4-18

Figure 4-19

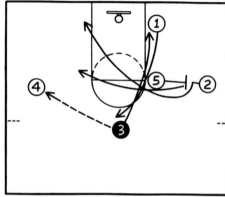

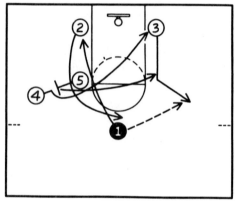

Figure 4-20

Figure 4-21

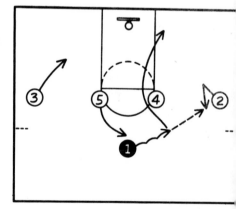

In Figure 4-19, 0-2, the first choice of 0-4, fakes down, drives his defensive man into 0-5, and cuts for the basket. 0-3 cuts right behind 0-2 as near to 0-5 as possible and forces his way down to the basket. As 0-3 cuts off 0-2, 0-5, the second choice of 0-4, cuts off 0-3 and breaks toward the ball to the medium post. As 0-5 cuts off 0-3, 0-1, the third choice of 0-4, cuts off 0-5 and breaks to the top of the key. 0-4 can pass the ball to 0-2, 0-5, or 0-1. If, upon receiving a pass from 0-4, 0-2, 0-1 or 0-5 have a shot they will shoot the ball. If the ball is passed out to 0-1 and 0-1 does not have a shot, then 0-1 initiates the shuffle play on the opposite side (Figure 4-20).

When this happens, 0-1 passes the ball to 0-3. 0-4, the first choice of 0-3, fakes down drives his defensive man into 0-5 and cuts for the basket. 0-1 cuts right behind 0-4 as near to 0-5 as possible and forces his way down to the basket. As 0-1 cuts off 0-4, 0-5, the second choice of 0-3, cuts off 0-1 and breaks to the medium post toward the ball. As 0-5 cuts off 0-1, 0-2, the third choice of 0-3, breaks out to the top of key. 0-3 can pass the ball to 0-4, 0-5, or 0-2.

If a shooting opportunity develops the shot is taken. If the ball is thrown out to 0-2 and he cannot shoot the ball, he starts the shuffle all over again on the opposite side. Once we go into the shuffle series we will continue running it until a shot is obtained.

This play, as was previously explained, came about because of the fact that 0-2 could not pass the ball to corner man 0-1 (Figure 4-18). The shuffle presented to you was not a set play. This action was not brought about by our own choosing, but was forced upon us by good, aggressive defensive play.

We have a set play from the corner alignment that we use after a time-out or as the first play at the start of a new quarter. It also has a shuffle flavor. We use it because we can get into it quickly and it hits fast, giving the defense little time to adjust. We find that after we run the play one time, the rest of our stuff goes better. It seems as if the opposing coach and his players worry about when we will employ the shuffle again, instead of concentrating on the plays we're running against them. We institute the play by telling our point man to go to the corner and shuffle. The biggest difference between the two shuffles is that in the pre-arranged set we make our off-side pivotman jump out to the top of the key to receive a pass from the wing man rather than have the off-side wing man come over to receive the ball (Figure 4-21). The off-side pivotman, by jumping out to the top of the key at times, helps keep his defensive man honest. It forces the defensive man into playing our pivotman closer and prevents him from sagging to the extent where he would be most effective.

In Figure 4-21, point man 0-1 puts the ball in play to 0-2 and cuts to the base of the foul line. Pivotman 0-5 moves out to the head of

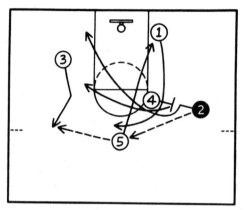

Figure 4-22   **Figure 4-23**

the key, wing man 0-3 moves toward the basket, and 0-4 positions himself to screen for 0-2.

In Figure 4-22, wing man 0-2 passes the ball out to the top of the key to pivotman 0-5; wing man 0-3 fakes down, then breaks out and receives a pass from 0-5. After 0-5 passes the ball to 0-3, 0-2, the first choice of 0-3, cuts off pivotman 0-4. Pivotman 0-5 moves down to the off side of the basket, cutting as close to 0-4 as possible. 0-4, the second choice of 0-3, cuts off 0-5 and breaks to the medium post towards the ball. 0-1, the third choice of 0-3, cuts off 0-4 and moves to the top of the key. 0-3 can pass the ball to 0-2, 0-5, or 0-1.

If the ball is passed out to 0-1, 0-1 will continue with the shuffle action of the opposite side of the court and the team will continue in this continuity until a shot is secured.

In Figure 4-22, the shuffle action depends upon 0-5's passing the ball to 0-3. If 0-5 has difficulty passing the ball to 0-3, 0-3 without any hesitation will come out and set a screen for 0-5 (Figure 4-23).

Wing man 0-3, unable to receive a pass from 0-5, comes out and sets a screen for 0-5. 0-3, after setting the screen, rolls to the basket. Pivotman 0-5 dribbles off the screen and shoots or passes to 0-3 rolling to the basket. 0-1 and 0-4 rebound the play and 0-2 drops back for defensive balance.

This concludes our discussion of the *Pass and Cut, Go to the Corner*. It also exhausts the cutting options of point man 0-1. The pass and cut game has proven very beneficial to us. The plays involved are easily learned, and help prepare your team for almost any eventuality. In our opinion they probably constitute the most important plays in our entire offense.

5

PLAY 3 AND PLAY 4:

SCREENING TOWARD THE BALL

The two plays already outlined were keyed by our point man's actions as a cutter. Plays 3 and 4 are keyed by our point man's action as a screener. Both plays will be keyed by our point man screening towards the ball for wing man 0-2. If our point man decides to enter into a screening game toward the ball, he can initiate a series of options by passing the ball to 0-2 and moving into a position either to the inside or the outside of 0-2. Whenever he elects to move to the inside of 0-2, it acts as a key for the execution of Play 3, which, with all of its options, will be referred to as the *Inside Screen*. Whenever our point man elects to move to the outside of 0-2, his actions again act as a key, but this time for the execution of Play 4, which, with all of its options, will be referred to as the *Outside Screen,* more commonly called by our players the *Go-Behind.*

PLAY 3: THE INSIDE SCREEN

The *Inside Screen* is another one of those plays that we would rather have our point man stay away from. We do not like the idea of having our point man set a screen for our wing man and create for the defense a double-team opportunity. Our wing men aren't usually good enough ball handlers to cope effectively with double-team situations as consistently as we demand. However, game films have indicated that the inside screen by a point man for a wing man is a natural and spontaneous action that frequently develops during the game. Because of such evidence, and in line with our philosophy of freedom of movement in any direction after passing the ball, and also in order to develop in our point man the assurance that no matter where he moves after passing the ball it is impossible for him to make a mistake, we have no alternative but to incorporate the *Inside Screen* into our offense. What we do, however, is practice the inside options earnestly, giving the impression to our wing man that the play is unstoppable, but at the same time discouraging our point man from running it. In this way if our point man mistakenly sets an inside screen during the course of the game, our chances of successful execution are fairly good.

I don't want to give the impression that the *Inside Screen* is a bad play. On the contrary, it is a good play, and the options from it are excellent. We discourage its use only from fear of the double team. I think that it should be emphasized that our position here is not one in which we are trying to sell the 1-4 offense to you. We are simply trying to present to you what we know about the 1-4, and it is our intention to include in our presentation its weak as well as its strong points.

The *Inside Screen* provides us with a number of options where wing man 0-2 can be set up for a shot. Some of the more fruitful ones include the following:

1. Option 1: A drive right.
2. Option 2: A drive left.
3. Option 3: Hit the pivot and split.

Option 1: A Drive Right

In Figure 5-1, 0-1 puts the ball in play to 0-2, who moves toward the basket, then breaks out to receive the pass. 0-1 passes the ball to 0-2, follows his pass, and sets an inside screen on defensive man X-2. 0-2 receives the pass, faces his defensive man, waits for 0-1 to set the screen, fakes left and drives hard to his right. 0-1, after 0-2 drives, cuts to the basket. If 0-2 can beat X-2 and X-4 picks him up, 0-2 should pass off to 0-4. If 0-2 cannot beat X-2 to the basket, he shoots the jumper or passes off to 0-1 cutting to the basket. 0-5 sinks to and rebounds the off side. 0-3 takes two steps out to protect defensively.

Option 2: A Drive Left

In Figure 5-2, 0-1 has already passed the ball to 0-2 and has set an inside screen on X-2. 0-2 takes a quick power thrust with his right

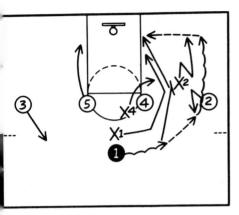

Figure 5-1

Figure 5-2

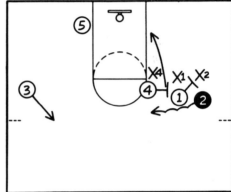

foot toward the baseline, takes a cross-over step to his left and drives left off the screen. If X-1 and X-2 do not switch, 0-2 should have a jump shot from the foul line. If the switch takes place, 0-2 should continue his drive left, forcing defensive man X-1 into 0-4's screen. If 0-2 has the shot or drive to the basket he makes use of the opportunity. If X-4 picks up 0-2, 0-2 should pass the ball to 0-4 rolling to the basket. 0-5 rebounds the off-side. 0-3 protects defensively and waits for possible interchange action with 0-2.

Option 3: Hit the Pivot and Split

In Figure 5-3, 0-1 puts the ball in play to 0-2. 0-2 moves toward basket, then breaks out to receive the pass. 0-1 passes to 0-2 and sets an inside screen for 0-2. 0-2 quickly passes the ball to 0-4. 0-1 breaks

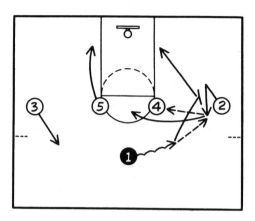

Figure 5-3

to the baseline side of 0-4 toward the basket. 0-2 cuts across the foul line in front of 0-4. 0-4 can pass to 0-1 or 0-2, shoot, or drive to the basket. 0-5 sinks to and rebounds the off side. 0-3 protects defensively.

PLAY 4: THE OUTSIDE SCREEN

Contrary to the use of the *Inside Screen,* we encourage the extensive use of the *Outside Screen.* In our presentation of the 1-4 offense, the *Outside Screen* or the *Go-Behind* is one of the strongest and most versatile plays we have to offer, and we recommend its use for the following reasons:

1. It enables us to take quick advantage of a height superiority. Whenever our wing man is bigger than the man defending against him, the play gives us an opportunity to get the ball to him in a floor position where it does the most good.
2. It gives us an opportunity to have our point man gain possession of the ball and yet have a live dribble left.
3. It makes it possible for us to set up our wing man for good percentage shots on the off side of the court.
4. It is a useful play whenever the defensive pivotman switches off defensively on horizontal screens (screens between the wing men and the pivotmen) but not against vertical screens (screens between the point man and the pivotman).

In Figure 5-4, point man 0-1 puts the ball in play to wing man 0-2.

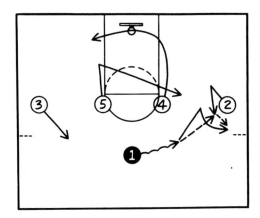

Figure 5-4

Wing man 0-2 moves down towards the basket, then breaks out to receive a pass from 0-1. 0-1 passes to 0-2, cuts to the inside of 0-2, calls the word "BACK," then drops behind 0-2. On the pass to 0-2, 0-4 breaks to the basket and clears to the opposite side. 0-5 breaks towards the ball to the high post; 0-3 takes two steps out to protect defensively; 0-4 rebounds the off side.

In Figure 5-4, it must be understood that when 0-2 gains possession of the ball, he doesn't necessarily have to give it back to point man 0-1. From this position, and before he hands the ball back to point man 0-1, 0-2 has the following options:

1. Option 1: Wing man 0-2 may drive the baseline.
2. Option 2: Wing man 0-2 may drive off pivotman 0-5.
3. Option 3: Wing man 0-2 may pass the ball to pivotman 0-5 and go behind him.
4. Option 4: Wing man 0-2 may pass the ball to 0-5 and set an inside screen for him.
5. Option 5: Wing man 0-2 may pass the ball to 0-5 and cut for the basket.

All of the options listed above have been previously outlined and discussed in detail. It is not necessary for us to discuss them here again. However, I hope that you will keep in mind that the options presented above are as important to the *Go-Behind* play as are the options that follow.

Option 6: Hit the Go Men

In Figure 5-5, 0-1 has already passed the ball to 0-2 and has taken his position behind 0-2. 0-2 drops the ball off to point man 0-1 standing behind him. 0-2 breaks across in front of 0-5 and cuts off his right side to the basket. 0-1 passes the ball to 0-2. Pivotman 0-5 sets a screen for 0-2, then rebounds. 0-4 rebounds the off side. Wing man 0-3 protects defensively.

In this play, 0-2 cuts off 0-5 because 0-2's defensive man insists upon placing himself between 0-2 and the ball. This means that 0-2's defensive man is behind 0-2, following him across to 0-5. If 0-2 cuts properly, he can beat his defensive man to the basket.

If 0-2's defensive man places himself between 0-2 and 0-5, 0-2 cuts to the basket as illustrated in Figure 5-6.

In this maneuver, 0-2, after passing the ball off to 0-1, moves over to 0-5, comes to a parallel stop, pivots counter-clockwise on his right foot, and cuts to the low post position. Whenever 0-2 is bigger than his defensive man, we make him go to the low post position and maneuver until he is clear enough to receive a pass from 0-1. Once 0-2 receives the ball he uses the power moves or the standard one-on-one moves.

It is unwise to hit the go man in the low post position whenever he is being guarded by a taller opponent. In such cases, if he cannot be hit as he is cutting towards the basket, he should not have the ball passed to him. It is much safer to have him clear to the opposite side of the court. This will force point man 0-1 to enter into Option 7.

Option 7: The Drive Off the Pivot

Once wing man 0-2 fails to receive the ball in the low post, he clears to the opposite side of the court (Figure 5-7). This sets the stage for pivotman 0-5 to enter into the play. Pivotman 0-5 must set a screen for point man 0-1. At this point let's stop for a moment to analyze the reason behind pivotman 0-5's screening for point man 0-1. Point man 0-1 is probably the smallest man on his team. Pivotman 0-5 is one of the largest. Point man 0-1 would probably be defended by an opponent who is in most cases the smallest man on his team. Since pivotman 0-5 is a big man, he must be defended against by someone of comparable size. If pivotman 0-5 sets a good enough screen for point

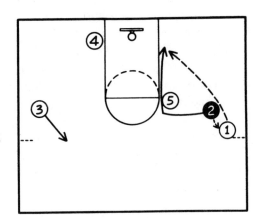

Figure 5-5

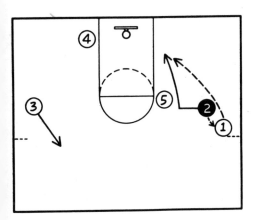

Figure 5-6

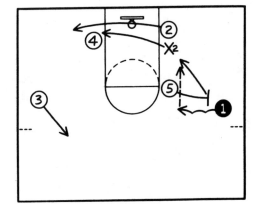

Figure 5-7

man 0-1, 0-5's defensive man has to pick up 0-1 driving or let him shoot from the foul line.

In most cases 0-5's defensive man picks up 0-1. Once this occurs 0-5 rolls to the basket. When 0-5 rolls to the basket he does so with 0-1's defensive man defending him. We now have 0-1, the smallest man on his team, being defended by 0-5's defensive man, who is one of the largest men on his team. Furthermore, we have 0-5, the largest man on his team, being defended by 0-1's defensive man, who is the smallest man on his team. It is quite evident that such a mismatch gives the offensive team a tremendous advantage.

There are only two ways that a defensive team can begin to cope with such a play:

1. 0-2's defensive man does not clear to the opposite side with him but stays in the low post on the strong side.
2. 0-5's defensive man employs a fake switch on point man 0-1 (Figure 5-8).

If in Figure 5-7, defensive man X-2 refuses to clear to the opposite side with 0-2, but instead holds up in the low post on the strong side to defend the screen and roll play between 0-1 and 0-5, 0-1 can neutralize such defensive action by automatically entering into our weakside series.

In Figure 5-8, X-5, in order to perform a fake switch, must go to the outside of 0-5. X-5 tries to slow up 0-1's dribble until X-1 is able to go over the top of 0-5 and pick up 0-1. To combat such a move 0-1 has to be alert. Whenever 0-1 is being screened for, he must focus his entire attention on the play of X-5. Each time he sees X-5 in such a position, he must yell "Cut" to 0-5. Just as soon as 0-5 hears the word "Cut" he releases the screen on X-1 and cuts to the basket. 0-5's move to the basket is taken with him facing the side line. In this instance 0-5 does not pivot and roll. He just makes a straight cut to the basket. 0-1 passes him the ball with 0-5 looking over his right shoulder.

Many times X-1, in positioning himself to go over the top of the screen set by 0-5, tends to forget that his main responsibility is to protect the baseline drive by 0-1. If 0-1 is not too anxious and waits for 0-5 to be stationary before he executes a power thrust, the baseline drive avails itself surprisingly often. If 0-1 drives right, 0-5 will cut for the basket. 0-1 has the opportunity to drive all the way, shoot the jump shot, or hit 0-5 cutting to the basket. We believe that the offensive maneuvers just discussed are more than adequate to cope with the aforementioned defensive adjustments that are sometimes employed against Option 7, the Drive Off the Pivot.

In Figure 5-5, 0-1 could possibly pass the ball to 0-5 instead of 0-2. Many times 0-5 is left undefended because his defensive man may be forced to help defend against the cut of 0-2 (Figure 5-9). When this happens 0-1 will pass the ball to 0-5. Whenever 0-1 passes to 0-5, he has two options:

1. Option 8: Pass to the pivot and go behind.
2. Option 9: Pass to the pivot and screen.

Both Options 8 and 9 have been previously outlined. Therefore in this chapter it won't be necessary for us to outline them again. Instead of outlining Options 8 and 9, let's consider 0-5's putting the ball in

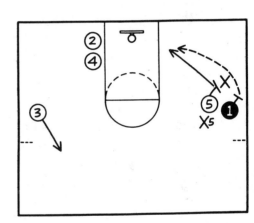

Figure 5-8

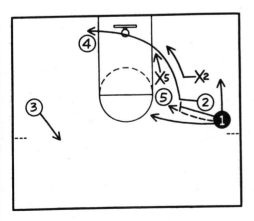

Figure 5-9

play on the weak-side because of the defensive play of X-5 and X-2 (Figure 5-9).

In this play, wing man 0-2 intiates his cut to the basket. If defensive man X-5 picks up 0-2 cutting for the basket, 0-5 will be clear. 0-1 then passes to 0-5, follows his pass and cuts in front of or behind 0-5. 0-4 rebounds the weak side and 0-3 takes two steps out to protect defensively.

If in Figure 5-10, 0-2 cannot shoot the ball after receiving a pass from 0-5, he waits for 0-4 to set a baseline screen. 0-2 will shoot the ball or pass it to 0-4 rolling. If 0-5 cannot pass the ball to 0-2, he will dribble it over to him, or 0-5 will pick up the ball and wait until 0-2 comes to get it on an interchange.

Option 10: Pass Out to the Point and Shuffle

In the play shown in Figure 5-9, I can't remember the last time 0-1 was forced to pass the ball out to the point position to key the start of the shuffle series. I don't believe it has ever occurred under game conditions. Nevertheless, in the event that it ever becomes necessary, I feel we must be adequately prepared.

The circumstances under which we would be forced to pass the ball out can only be brought about by a double team on 0-1 (Figure 5-11).

In this situation, after 0-1 is in possession of the ball, 0-2 cuts to the low post. Instead of 0-2's defensive man X-2 following 0-2 to the low post, he attempts to double-team 0-1. 0-2 in the low post is free. Therefore, he would not be forced to clear to the opposite side. The only time 0-2 will clear to the opposite side is when he is adequately defended. Without a defender defending him, he will remain in the low post position indefinitely. From such a position 0-2 has an easy scoring opportunity, provided 0-1 can get him the ball. If 0-1 fails to get 0-2 the ball and is forced to pass the ball out, 0-2's floor position is exactly the position we must have occupied for us to properly execute the shuffle. If a shot is not forthcoming on our first shuffle attempt, we will stay with the continuity until a shot is secured.

With the conclusion of Option 10, point man 0-1 has exhausted all the opportunities that can be derived from his passing to 0-2 and screening in the direction of the ball.

If 0-1 is going to be further utilized as a screener after he passes to 0-2, he has no alternative but to screen for someone other than 0-2.

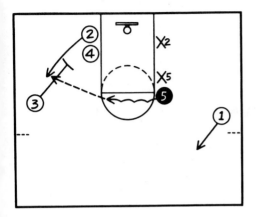

Figure 5-10

Figure 5-11

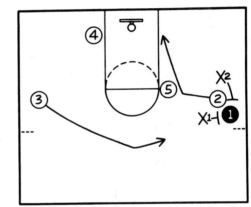

We refer to such screens as screens away from the ball. Those screens and the offensive opportunities derived from them will be outlined in Chapter 6.

6

PLAY 5 AND PLAY 6: PASS AND

SCREEN AWAY FROM THE BALL

Most high school basketball teams have two coaches: the head coach and one assistant. In some of the more fortunate and affluent schools, the number of coaches per team can be as high as three or four. In some of the less fortunate situations one coach may be responsible for coaching the entire basketball program. Whatever the situation, the responsibility of coaching a team is a heavy burden to assume.

The times we allot to the various responsibilities vary from coach to coach, depending upon the situation in which the coach must perform his duties and the caliber of his players. The more help a coach has, the more basketball he is likely to get across to his players. The better his personnel, the more sophisticated the offenses and defenses he can use.

Some coaches find themselves teaching shooting, dribbling, and passing day after day. Most of their time must be taken up with such chores when they have players who can not shoot, dribble, or pass. When coaches have players who can perform these fundamentals well, they can afford to spend shorter periods of time on such basics.

Whatever the situation of the coach, when game time comes and the game is in progress, his value to his team is determined by how well he has utilized his coaching time. Coaches are paid to coach, not to cheer, argue, or perform. The coach who makes good use of his time may not always win, but he must always be beaten—he will never beat himself. During the course of a ball game, one of the jobs the coach is being paid for is his alertness to the various defenses his team is facing. He must understand the defense confronting his team and be in a position to counteract it with some offensive tactic. If his regular offense is having difficulty securing good shots, it must be because of some unusual defensive deployment. The coach must be able to recognize the man who is clogging up his offense and have something in his offensive arsenal to combat that man's play.

For such situations we offer our screening series away from the ball, composed of plays not in themselves very strong. However, these plays, if used under the conditions outlined earlier, may just be enough to force your opponent into abandoning his special defense, thus forcing him to move into a more conventional one with which the team's main offense can successfully cope.

These plays can force opposing teams out of unconventional defenses because they're designed to:

1. Free an off-side wing man or pivotman for a shot.
2. Provide setups and clear outs to take advantage of various one-on-one moves.
3. Control defensive support by the off-side wing man or pivotman.

Our screening series away from the ball involves our point man passing to a wing man. Instead of following the path of the ball, he moves away from the pass receiver and screens for an off-side wing man or pivotman (Figure 6-1).

PLAY 5: SCREEN FOR THE OFF-SIDE WING MAN

The *Screen for the Off-Side Wing Man* is employed to take advantage of the defensive play of 0-3's defensive man, X-3 (Figure 6-1).

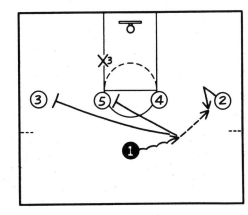

Figure 6-1

In Figure 6-2, if 0-2 were to drive the baseline and succeed in beating his defensive man, X-3 would undoubtedly offer some support defensively that would obstruct 0-2 in shooting the lay-up shot.

If 0-2 were to drive off pivotman 0-4, 0-1's defensive man, X-1 would offer enough defensive support to impede 0-2's progress toward the basket. In both cases, even if 0-2 was successful in beating X-2 one-on-one, the support defense of X-3 and X-1 would have limited him to at least a hurried jump shot.

In our screening series away from the ball, if 0-1, after passing to 0-2, would come to the inside of 0-3, X-1 and X-3 would be prompted to move from the defensive positions they are occupying in Figure 6-2 to the defensive positions illustrated in Figure 6-3.

In Figure 6-3, whenever 0-1 screens for 0-3, 0-2 can now drive the baseline if he can beat X-2 in that direction one-on-one. Whenever

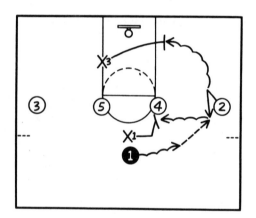

Figure 6-2

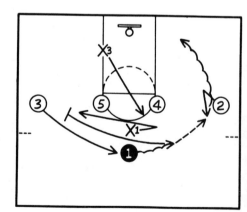

Figure 6-3

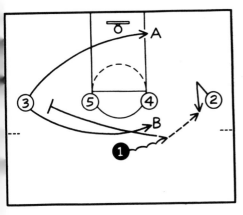

Figure 6-4

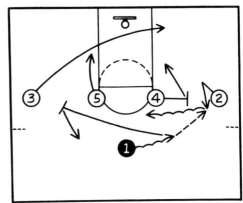

Figure 6-5

0-1 passes to 0-2 and screens for 0-3, 0-3 has two cutting routes, A and B, that he can follow (Figure 6-4).

If 0-3 follows Route A, 0-2 has two options:

Option 1: Drive off the pivot.
Option 2: Pass the ball to the off-side wing man in the low post.

Option 1: Wing Man Drives Off the Pivot

Figure 6-5 illustrates Option 1.

Option 2: Hit the Wing Man in the Low Post

In Figure 6-6 wing man 0-3 attempts to follow Route A. If 0-3 is clear, 0-2 will pass him the ball. If 0-3 is covered, 0-2 will drive off

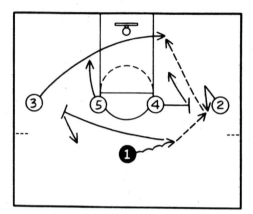

Figure 6-6

Figure 6-7

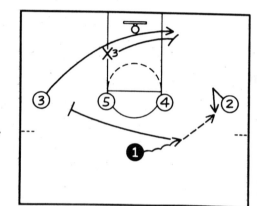

pivotman 0-4 (Figure 6-5). In both figures 0-1 must pass the ball to 0-2 and go away from the ball. To set a screen for 0-2, pivotman 0-4 sets an inside screen for 0-2, then rolls to the basket; pivotman 0-5 sinks to and rebounds the off side; and 0-1, after screening for 0-3, takes two steps out and protects defensively.

To succeed Options 1 and 2 are dependent upon each other. Option 1 is an outgrowth of Option 2. If in Figure 6-5, 0-2 cannot pass to 0-3 cutting to the low post, he can immediately enter into Option 1 by driving off pivotman 0-4.

Although Option 1 and Option 2 are dependent upon each other, the controlling mechanism governing the play to be run is defensive man X-3 (Figure 6-7). In this play, if 0-3 has X-3 beaten, then 0-2 should pass 0-3 the ball. If X-3 has 0-3 beaten, then 0-2 should enter into Option 1.

Now that Options 1 and 2 have been presented, we must not forget why this series of screening away from the ball has been instituted.

In Figure 6-7, the route of 0-3, considering the sagging of X-3, is the poorest route he could possibly follow. 0-3 has little chance of securing the ball from wing man 0-2 with X-3 occupying such a position. If 0-3 follows the above route, 0-2 should automatically enter into Option 1, even though the objective of our screening away from the ball series was to alter X-3's play and keep him from sagging. If 0-3 follows this route to the low post, 0-3 has failed to force X-3 out of the defensive pattern we want altered. In such instances 0-3, by moving himself into a position close to X-3, makes it possible for X-3 to sag sufficiently to clog up the right side and discourage 0-2 from passing the ball to 0-3. Such a move by 0-3 only makes it easier for X-3 to carry out his defensive assignment. To alter X-3's defensive position, we recommend that 0-3 follow the route illustrated in Figure 6-8.

In this situation, when 0-3 routes himself to the head of the key, X-3 cannot remain in the position indicated. X-3 is forced to come out from this position to a position at the head of the key where he can effectively keep 0-3 from shooting or defend against a shot taken. Such a movement effectively interrupts X-3's defensive sag pattern. If X-3 does not come out to defend against 0-3, 0-2 passes 0-3 the ball for a nice, easy shot. I guarantee that X-3 will eventually come out to pick up 0-3, and the objective of our screen away from the ball will be realized.

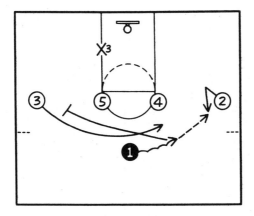

Figure 6-8

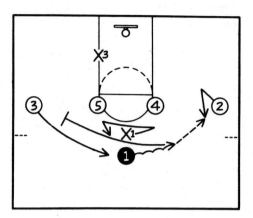

Figure 6-9

Figure 6-10

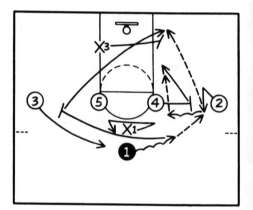

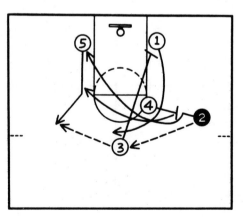

Figure 6-11

Even if 0-3 moves to the top of the key, X-3 can remain in his sag position by switching men defensively (Figure 6-9).

Here, because of the defensive switch, X-3's defensive position has not been altered. X-3 can still clog up the middle, effectively restraining Option 1 and Option 2. The responsibility for combating the switching play of X-3 and X-1 rests with 0-1. Whenever 0-1 moves over to screen or change positions with 0-3 and the switch on defense occurs, 0-1 must immediately cut to the low post position on the ball side of the floor (Figure 6-10).

In this situation, X-3's defensive position has not been altered. His floor position would render Option 2 initially ineffective. If 0-2 chooses to execute Option 1, X-1 would shut off his drive and X-3 would intercede in an attempted pass to 0-4 rolling. Both options have been adequately defended.

Option 3: Pass the Ball Out

If 0-2 finds himself in such a predicament, he must pass the ball out, keying our shuffle series (Figure 6-11).

When 0-1 breaks to the top of the key, X-3's sagging pattern is effective. X-3 must move out to the top of the key with 0-1. Thus, in our screen away from the ball series, the shuffle from the above alignment helps achieve the desired objectives. We will continue to shuffle until a shot is obtained.

If in Figure 6-11, 0-2 cannot pass the ball to 0-3, then he may motion 0-1 to the corner to receive a pass and enter into Option 4.

Option 4: Hit the Screener in the Corner and Clear

In Figure 6-12, 0-1 can:

1. Pass the ball to 0-2 cutting.
2. Wait for 0-4 to set a screen and enter into the screen and roll play.

If 0-1 cannot shoot or pass the ball, he must dribble the ball across the foul line toward 0-3 and enter into our weak-side series (Figure 6-13).

In this play, 0-3 screens down for 0-2, and 0-1 passes the ball to 0-2 for a shot. If 0-2 cannot shoot, 0-5 will enter into the play by

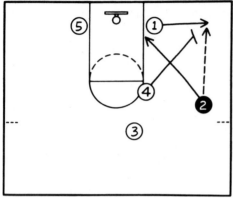

Figure 6-12

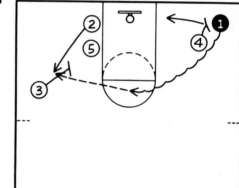

Figure 6-13

setting a baseline screen for him. 0-5, after screening, rolls to the basket. 0-4 rebounds the off side and 0-1 protects defensively.

PLAY 6: SCREEN FOR THE OFF-SIDE PIVOT

In analyzing the 1-4 alignment (Figure 6-14), there is a strong possibility that on a pass from 0-1 to 0-2, 0-5's defensive man X-5 can be instructed to sag to a floor position where he can lend the support necessary to stop our regular 1-4 offense.

In such situations our screen away from the ball series is flexible enough to be used here in the same manner as we did in Play 5, *Screen for the Off-Side Wing Man.* This type of defensive support play by X-5 is a bigger, more dangerous defensive gamble than the support offered by 0-3's defensive man, X-3. X-3 guarding 0-3 has little to lose if, after 0-1 enacts the key for passing the ball to 0-2, 0-1 decides to pick up his dribble quickly or suddenly reverses his dribble and passes the ball to 0-3 (Figure 6-15). From such a floor position 0-3, after receiving a pass from 0-1, does not present an immediate scoring threat. In fact, a shot by 0-3 from such a floor position is probably his poorest percentage shot. Defensive man X-3 would most likely encourage 0-3 to shoot the ball rather than discourage such a shot.

Under similar conditions, X-5 would be making a grave defensive error if he were to allow 0-5, occupying the floor position indicated,

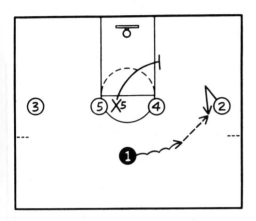

Figure 6-14

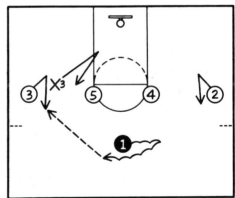

Figure 6-15

to receive a pass from 0-1 (Figure 6-16). Here, once 0-5 has possession of the ball, he has a great percentage shot. From such a floor position X-5 could ill afford to encourage 0-5 to shoot the ball.

In comparing the two defensive support maneuvers, we would prefer X-5 rather than X-3 to offer the support. X-5's support enables us to do many more things faster and with better results. This is mainly due to the fact that 0-5 is much closer to the basket and, consequently,

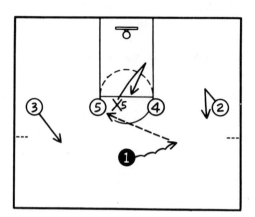

Figure 6-16

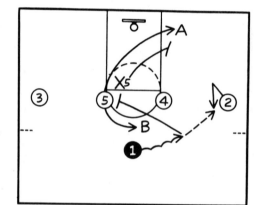

Figure 6-17

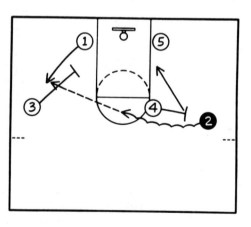

Figure 6-18

is a greater scoring threat. In Figure 6-17, whenever 0-1 passes the ball to 0-2 and screens for 0-5, 0-5 has the two cutting routes illustrated.

0-2 has the Option of hitting 0-5 at A, or if 0-5 follows Route B, 0-2 will pass him the ball at B.

If 0-5 follows Route A and 0-2 cannot pass him the ball, 0-4 will enter into the play by setting a screen for 0-2 (Figure 6-18). With pivotman 0-5 in the position indicated, the screen and roll between 0-4 and 0-2 will be ineffective. 0-2, then, should either shoot the ball or enter into the weak-side series. Once 0-3 realizes that 0-2 is entering into the weak-side series he will screen down for 0-1.

Now and then in Figure 6-17 we are able to get the ball into 0-5 for an easy shot. Mostly, however, it sets up 0-2 for a good shot (Figure 6-18).

I must admit that the weak-side series has also been fruitful; however, the play does not alter the defensive sag and support defense of X-5 (Figure 6-14). Since the objective of the screen away from the ball series is to alter this type of defensive play, Route A for such purposes is of little value. Let's explore for such purposes the merits of having 0-5 follow Route B.

In Figure 6-17, whenever 0-5 follows Route B, 0-5 ends up in the point position. In the event 0-5 receives a pass from 0-2, X-5 has to move out to discourage 0-5 from shooting. If X-5 fails to do so, 0-5 shoots the ball. You can readily see that very few teams will take the

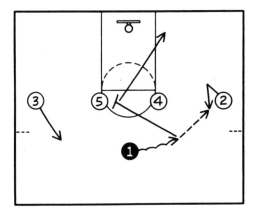

Figure 6-19

chance of sagging X-5 at the expense of giving up this shot to 0-5. Most teams, after the first clear shot by 0-5, will stop sagging X-5, and have him, from that point on, stay with 0-5. When this occurs, the screen away from the ball series has accomplished its objective. When teams begin to follow 0-5 to the top of the key, 0-1, after the screen for 0-5, will cut to the low post position towards the ball (Figure 6-19). From such an alignment, if 0-2 cannot pass the ball to 0-1, 0-2 will pass the ball out to 0-5. This pass-out serves as the key for enacting the shuffle series which has been previously explained.

With the conclusion of the shuffle play, we have exhausted every available cut to the basket, screen towards the ball, and screen away from the ball that can be made by point man 0-1 after passing to wing man 0-2. We are now ready to investigate, in Chapter 7, the opportunities that can arise from a pass by the point man to the pivotman.

7

PLAY 7:

HIT THE PIVOT

The big offensive play in any offense consistently involves a pass into the pivot. It matters little whether or not your pivotman is used primarily as a shooter or as a feeder. To win, you must get him the ball no matter what type offense you advocate; it's imperative that you work hard on finding ways and means to accomplish this end. In this respect 1-4 people have a definite and clear-cut advantage over all other types of offensive alignments. The double pivot alignment of the 1-4 offers twice as many opportunities to get the ball into the pivot as do the more conventional alignments of the 2-3, 1-3-1, or 1-2-2.

With two pivotmen available to pass the ball to, our point men are instructed to try to get the ball into one or the other each time they bring the ball down court. They are instructed not to put the ball in play to a wing man until they find it impossible to complete a pass to either one of the two pivotmen available.

More often than not our point man fails to get the ball to a pivotman. Usually the major responsibility for such failures has to be shouldered by the pivotman and not by the point man. We take the stand that it is up to the pivotmen not only to get themselves open, but also to be clear at the right time and in a floor position not too distant from the floor position of the point man.

If the pivotman fails to clear himself properly, he cannot expect to receive the ball. The most frequent and most dangerous mistake made by our pivotmen is that through impatience they clear themselves before our point man is in the proper floor position. Unfortunately, they invite our point man into chancing too long a pass, which usually ends up by being intercepted by the pivotman's defender. Even when these passes succeed, the point man should be highly criticized for engaging in such actions. In situations like this the point man can never gamble. He must be absolutely sure that his passes to the pivot will not be intercepted. A bad pass by the point man is more than just a bad pass. Almost every time one of his passes is intercepted, the opposing team has an easy two points. The 1-4 offense is not geared to stop defensively the fast break that develops from such interceptions. With our point man moving to some new position each time he passes the ball, there is no way he can successfully protect against a fast break resulting from the interception of one of his passes. Consequently we make him develop an attitude of being sure rather than sorry. If he occasionally passes up a pivotman who is clear, I refuse to question his judgment. I will criticize him severely if he attempts a pass into a pivotman and the ball is intercepted, but I refuse to make any comment when he fails to pass the ball to a pivotman standing clear. It is easy to understand that we have a real need for some sort of gauge to govern the actions of both pivotmen and the point man whenever the point man is trying to pass the ball into one of them. The pivotmen must have ways and means of freeing themselves at the exact instant that the point man looks for them to be open. The point man, on the other hand, must have some procedure to follow when he becomes aware of the pivotman's freeing action. We solve both problems by making sure the pivotmen do not start their freeing moves until after the point man crosses the mid-court jumping circle. The point man has to be somewhere between the two jump ball circles before the pivot-men move (Figure 7-1).

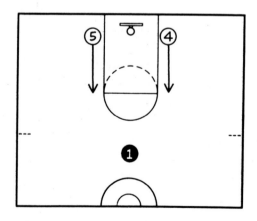

Figure 7-1

As the point man brings the ball up court, he should have his eyes glued on both pivotmen. The point man's cue that he is ready to pass the ball into a clear pivotman occurs just as soon as the point man crosses the mid-court, jump-ball circle. No matter how clear a pivotman standing in the pivot may be, we never want the point man to chance a pass to him before reaching this floor position.

With the establishment of regulations governing the pass to the pivot from the point man, we can now discuss the various ways that 1-4 pivotmen go about clearing themselves for receiving such a pass.

Our pivotmen have several different alignments and movements they can enter into that are designed to aid in freeing themselves for the purpose of receiving a pass from the point man. If in the 1-4 offense the objective is to hit the pivotmen each time the ball is put in play, it stands to reason that they cannot continually repeat the same clearing action throughout the game. They must have several options available to them to help keep the defense occupied and guessing at all times. Some of the various movements our pivotmen employ are:

1. A break out from the low post.
2. Low post screens.
3. A cross.
4. A high-low screen.
5. A stack.

As the point man is bringing the ball down court and enters the prescribed floor position for passing the ball into the pivotman, our pivotmen by pre-arrangement enter into one of these five maneuvers. One of our pivotmen is given the responsibility for declaring what alignment and what movements will be used. The best way to understand these movements is to consider them as a separate offense. I think they can be viewed as a pivotman's offense that is completely independent of our regular 1-4. Such an offense affects only pivotmen. Their movements have no effect on the plays we have presented thus far. They have no effect on what play the point man is going to run other than the fact that the pointman will throw the ball into one of the pivotmen if he happens to be clear. The wing men need not concern themselves with what the pivotmen are doing because their movements do not affect the wing man's play. The wing men's play remains constant on each of our plays, and is not determined by the five pivotmen maneuvers listed above. The wing men's actions are determined only by the maneuvers of the point man.

The Break Out from the Low Post

In Figure 7-2, once point man 0-1 crosses the mid-court jump-ball circle, pivotmen 0-5 and 0-4 take a short jab step with their inside foot toward the basket. Just as soon as they complete this jab step they push off that foot and break out toward the high post position as fast as possible. Once they get to the high post position they come to a jump stop, preferably with their feet straddling the foul circle. If 0-5 or 0-4 is clear, point man 0-1 should pass the ball so that it is received as the pivotman is completing his jump stop. The ball should be passed toward the arm of the pivotman farthest away from his defensive man.

The Low Post Screens

In Figure 7-3, once point man 0-1 crosses the mid-court jump-ball circle, pivotmen 0-5 and 0-4 interchange positions. Once they interchange they break out to the high post position, stopping in the manner and floor position described previously.

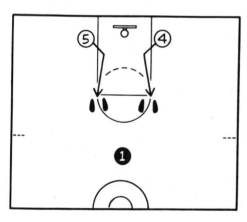

Figure 7-2

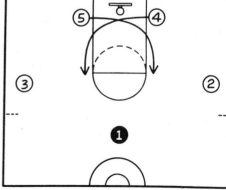

Figure 7-3

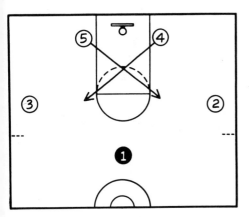

Figure 7-4

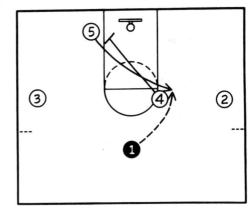

Figure 7-5

The Cross or X

In Figure 7-4, once point man 0-1 crosses the mid-court jump-ball circle, pivotmen 0-5 and 0-4 break out diagonally to the high post positions on opposite sides of the court. This particular maneuver is used extensively whenever we are fortunate enough to have a center whom we can depend upon and employ primarily as a scorer.

The High-Low Screen

The high-low screen is another maneuver we employ whenever we want to get the ball into a high scoring center. This maneuver is employed from a 1-3-1 alignment. The pivotman to whom the ball is to go must occupy the baseline position (Figure 7-5).

After employing the high-low screen a few times, we usually force the defense to start switching every time 0-4 screens for 0-5. 0-4's defensive man will pick up 0-5, and 0-5's defensive man will pick up 0-4. In such situations, if 0-5 continues to pursue his diagonal cut to the pivot position on the opposite side of the court, the high-low screen is usually ineffective because 0-4's defensive man will keep 0-5 from getting the ball. Whenever our pivotmen are confronted with such a switch, 0-5 must change the direction of his cut. Instead of cutting diagonally across the foul lane to the high post on the opposite side, he should follow the route illustrated in Figure 7-6.

When 0-5 changes the direction of his cut, he has X-4 beaten, and it is relatively simple for 0-1 to pass the ball safely to 0-5.

The Stack

The stack alignment is a special alignment that we employ to take advantage of a defensive man who is in foul trouble. In Figure 7-7, if

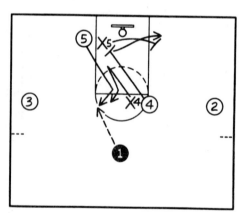

Figure 7-6

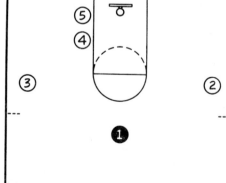

Figure 7-7

0-2 has his defensive man in such a circumstance, this alignment makes it possible for 0-2 to have plenty of room to play one-on-one on his side of the court. If 0-3's defensive man is in a similar situation, our two pivotmen would stack on the right side. To keep the defensive pivotmen honest, we have a set of screens we use from this alignment designed to free a pivotman. If the defensive men defending against our pivotman do not switch, our pivotman will follow the procedure illustrated in Figure 7-8. If the defensive men switch, our pivotmen follow the procedure illustrated in Figure 7-9.

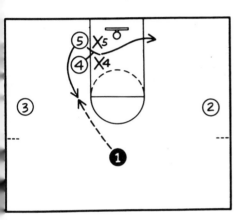

Figure 7-8

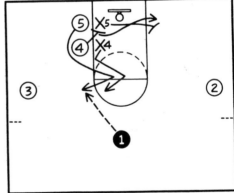

Figure 7-9

PLAY 7: HIT THE PIVOT

Having described the various methods we employ in our offense to clear a pivotman for receiving a pass, we will now consider Play 7, *Hit the Pivot*. This play, with all its options, is based upon the pivotman's use of the break-out maneuver from the low post position.

Play 7, *Hit the Pivot*, is perhaps the strongest play in our entire 1-4 offense. Because of its strength our point man is instructed to try to execute this play every time he brings the ball down court. Only after he decides he cannot successfully pass the ball to the pivot does he attempt to execute another play. Theoretically, if we were ever able to play a perfect offensive game, the entire game would be played with an offense consisting of this one play. The play is built upon and employs the use of some the most outstanding offensive concepts ever developed from the game. The play includes and deals with such concepts as:

1. The cutting game against pressure defenses.
2. The clear out.
3. The one-on-one game.
4. The employment of the second guard.
5. The screening game (baseline screens, vertical screens, horizontal screens, and stationary screens).
6. The interchange series.
7. The continuity series of play.
8. The off-side series of play.
9. The off-side rebounding.

Option 1: Pass to the On-Side Wing Man

Rule: Wing men must cut to the basket and clear to the opposite side every time the pivotman on the same side of the court receives a pass.

In Figure 7-10, once 0-1 crosses the mid-court jump-ball circle, pivotmen 0-5 and 0-4 break out to their high post positions. Point man 0-1 passes the ball to 0-4, breaks up inside the foul circle, plants his right foot, then screens for 0-3. 0-2, after 0-4 receives the ball, cuts back door (behind his defensive man) to the basket. 0-4 passes the ball to 0-2 cutting. 0-3 breaks off the screen set by 0-1 and moves to the top of the key. 0-5 rebounds the off side and 0-4 the strong side. The backdoor cut is most effective against pressure defenses. Our point man is instructed to enter into Play 7, *Hit the Pivot*, just as soon as he becomes aware that our wing man is being overplayed.

When 0-2, in Figure 7-10, is being overplayed, he usually has his man beat on his cut to the basket. The only defensive man that could possibly contain him would be X-5, the man guarding 0-5 (Figure

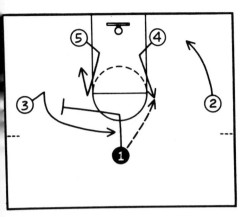

Figure 7-10

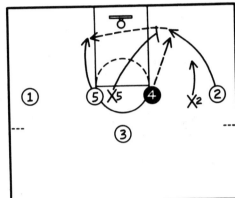

Figure 7-11

7-11). When X-5 moves over to offer his defensive support on 0-2, 0-2 will pass the ball to 0-5 under.

Option 2: Go One-on-One

Like most coaches, we spend many hours each season practicing our one-on-one moves. Unless we provide opportunities in our offense for our players to use these one-on-one moves, all the time spent on teaching and practicing them has been wasted.

Play 7 is designed to take advantage of all the one-on-one moves our pivotmen can execute. Our 1-4 offense makes it possible for our pivotmen to execute their moves by clearing the wing man to the opposite side. In Figure 7-10, just as soon as pivotman 0-4 receives the ball from point man 0-1, he looks for 0-2 cutting to the basket. First, he looks to see if 0-2 is clear on his cut. Second, he looks over his outside shoulder at 0-2; he should be able to see where his defensive man is located as well. If 0-4, after receiving the ball, looks over his left shoulder and sees that his defensive man is not protecting against a possible baseline drive, 0-4 will immediately execute a power right

103

with his back to the basket (Figure 7-12). This power move takes precedence over Option 1, a pass to 0-2 cutting back door.

If in Figure 7-12, X-4 moves over to the baseline side of 0-4, 0-4, when looking over his shoulder for 0-2 cutting, should be aware of X-4's position. In such a situation 0-4 should execute a power left with his back to the basket (Figure 7-13).

The power left with the back to the basket and the power right with the back to the basket are moves that should be executed almost as soon as pivotman 0-4 receives the ball. The pivotmen must recognize these two situations and be able to use them to take advantage of such defensive errors. It is highly possible that 0-4's defensive man X-4 positions himself so that 0-4 is discouraged from driving in any direction with his back to the basket. This situation usually occurs every time our pivotman is in possession of the ball with his back to the basket and X-4 has positioned himself in such a manner that 0-4 cannot feel him close by with his backside. We tell our pivotman that whenever he cannot feel the defensive man with his backside, he must turn and face him. Before our pivotmen turn to face their defensive men, they must be absolutely sure that the wing man cutting is not open and that he has cleared to the opposite side (Figure 7-14).

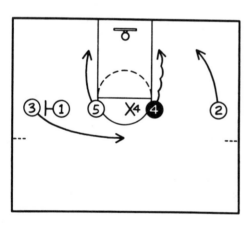

Figure 7-12

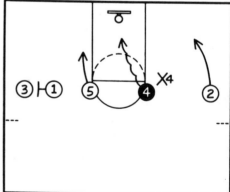

Figure 7-13

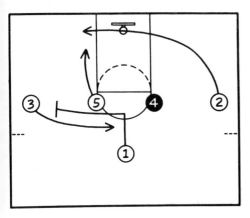

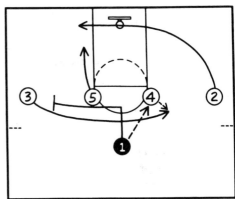

Figure 7-14

Figure 7-15

In this situation, after 0-2 clears to the opposite side pivotman 0-4 has the entire right side clear for him to play one-on-one against his defensive man. Here he can turn and face his defensive man, execute a power thrust, drive the baseline, shoot a jump shot, execute a power move, or drive left with use of a cross-over. The point we are trying to make is that in the execution of the play, we've given the pivotman an opportunity to use any free-lance moves that he can execute with some degree of efficiency.

Option 3: Pass to the Point

Even though we spend considerable time trying to develop good one-on-one moves, they cannot always be used in a game. Sometimes our pivotmen are up against defensive men who are unusually tall or unusually good players. In cases where our pivotman may not feel capable of beating his defensive man one-on-one, it is not mandatory for him to try to beat his defensive man. He can hold on to the ball and enter into Option 3.

Figure 7-15 illustrates Option 3, Pass to the Point. Here 0-1 passes to 0-4, then screens away from the ball for wing man 0-3. Wing man

0-2 clears to the opposite side. Pivotman 0-4 cannot pass to 0-2 or play one-on-one against his defensive man, so his next move is to look for 0-3. 0-3 cuts off the screen set for him by 0-1, moves toward 0-4, receives the ball and drives or shoots the jumper. 0-2 and 0-5 rebound the off side. Point man 0-1 protects defensively.

Frequently, after our point man passes the ball into the pivot and moves over to screen for 0-3, 0-1's defensive man becomes careless. When he does and our point man becomes aware of his actions, 0-1 varies his movements as shown in Figure 7-16.

Here point man 0-1 can vary his assignment without altering the play of his teammates. Point man 0-1 has the option then of setting himself up for a shot or setting one up for 0-3. Once point man 0-1 breaks inside the foul circle, he can plant his feet in such a manner that he can move in any direction. The direction he pursues depends upon the position of his defensive man. If his defensive man has taken a step toward 0-4, 0-1 should screen for 0-3. If 0-1's defensive man fails to take such a step, and instead decides to play 0-1 head on, 0-1 should plant his left foot and cut behind 0-4 to gain possession of the ball.

The variation employed here by 0-1 is another example of how our 1-4 offense takes advantage of a free-lance move. However, even though the move is free-lance in nature, once it enters into our offense we have control over it. Here again this play typifies the controlled free-lance style of play we advocate in our 1-4 offense.

Option 4: The Off-Side Series

In Figures 7-15 and 7-16, if pivotman 0-4 fails to hand the ball off, he must immediately look to the weak side and enter into Option 4, the weak-side series (Figure 7-17).

In this play, pivotman 0-4 enacts the key for initiating the weak-side series by dribbling the ball toward 0-3 with his back to the basket and sliding his feet across the foul line. 0-3 and 0-5 screen down for 0-2. 0-4 passes to 0-2 and the weak-side series is implemented.

If in Figure 7-17, pivotman 0-4 cannot pass the ball to wing man 0-2 cutting off the double screen, 0-4 will carry the ball over to him with a dribble handing the ball off as they interchange, and 0-2 can shoot, drive or play with 0-1. As was said earlier, Play 7, *Hit the Pivot,* with all its options, is one of our strongest plays. Almost every time we get the ball to the pivotman, we get some kind of shot.

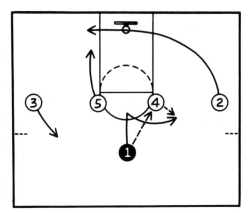

Figure 7-16

Figure 7-17

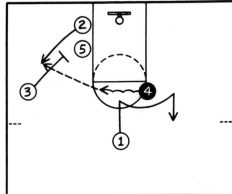

When we do not succeed it is usually due to poor passing. The one defensive man we must recognize as the one causing these bad passes is point man 0-1's defensive man. Many times 0-1's defensive man will double-up on our pivotman. When he does he can cause our man to throw the ball away, he can tie him up with the ball, or he can steal the ball completely. Our pivotman must always be aware of the little mice, as we call them, gnawing at the ball. To combat such defensive play once it is encountered, we ask our pivotmen to look immediately to the off-side. In Figure 7-18, 0-1's defensive man X-1 doubles up on pivotman 0-4. If X-1 doubles up on 0-4, 0-1 should be open. Pivotman 0-4 should throw 0-1 the ball. 0-1 can shoot, drive, or initiate the weak-side series by passing to 0-2.

If 0-2 cannot shoot the ball, pivotman 0-5 will set a baseline screen for him. If point man 0-1 cannot pass the ball to 0-2, 0-1 can carry the ball to him with a dribble, handing him the ball after an inter-change.

This concludes our discussion of Play 7, *Hit the Pivot*. With its con-clusion we have exhausted every possible passing outlet available to

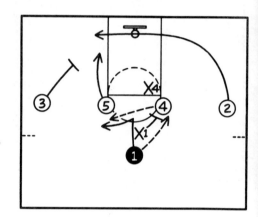

Figure 7-18

our point man. We have now completed the development of our offense from a pass, and shall enter into the offensive plays used in our 1-4 offense that are initiated from a dribble.

8

PLAY 8:

THE GO PLAY

Once our point man is put in a position where he cannot safely initiate our offense by means of a shot, drive, or pass, he has no other choice but to attempt its implementation by means of a dribble.

The dribble in our 1-4 offense is used primarily as a substitute for a pass, usually replacing the pass between the point man and the wing man. You will recall that the point man has been instructed to try to put the ball in play to a pivotman after he brings the ball down court. If he cannot put the ball in play to a pivotman, his second alternative is to put the ball into play with a pass to a wing man. It is only after our point man cannot pass the ball to a wing man that he engages the use of the dribble, his third alternative.

Since the key for passing the ball to a wing man is the point man dribbling the ball toward one of the wings, it is evident that a different key for implementing the offense by means of a dribble is needed. The key enacted verbally as the point man is dribbling the ball to the wing position is the word "Go." Consequently, we have decided to call Play 8 the *Go Play*.

The *Go Play* in our 1-4 offense is a very important play. Unlike any one of the other plays presented, it cannot be excluded from our offense. Without its inclusion, the 1-4 could not possibly be a successful offense. It is important to our offense in a number of ways, but the three most important are:

1. It makes it possible for us to get the ball to a wing man who is closely guarded.

2. It provides a means for a wing man enjoying a height superiority to take full advantage of a mismatch.
3. It makes it possible for us to control the defense by preventing them from double-teaming our point man.

Option 1: Pass to the Wing Man in the First Low Post Position

In Figure 8-1, 0-1 dribbles towards wing man 0-2 and calls out the word "Go." Wing man 0-2 clears to the low post position, then pivots to receive a pass from 0-1 at the right wing position. 0-2 can shoot or play one-on-one with his defensive man. 0-5 watches the plan develop, then sinks to and rebounds the off side. Pivotman 0-4 will rebound if 0-2 shoots. 0-3 takes two steps out to protect defensively.

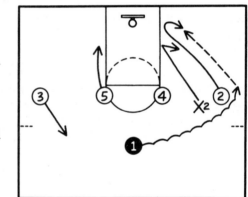

Figure 8-1

Option 1, in Figure 8-1, is a seemingly simple maneuver. You may doubt that such a maneuver could possibly free a closely guarded wing man. You may find it hard to understand how such a simple maneuver makes it possible for us to take advantage of a height mismatch. Perhaps you may have misgivings as to how such action really helps control the defense to such an extent that it is impossible for them to effectively double-team our point man.

If you will just bear with me, I guarantee I can prove to you that the play will effectively handle any one of the three situations described independent of each other, or all three collectively, as they arise. Let's begin our discussion with an explanation as to how Option 1 of the Go Play prevents our point man from getting double-teamed.

If in Figure 8-1, 0-1 is to be double-teamed, the man most likely to perform the double team would be 0-2's defensive man. To prevent 0-2's defensive man from doubling up on point man 0-1, 0-2 is instructed to move away from 0-1 as he dribbles toward him. There should always be a distance of about eight feet between point man 0-1 dribbling the ball and wing man 0-2. If this rule is adhered to, point man 0-1 and wing man 0-2 always have sufficient distance between them to deter 0-2's defensive man from entering into a double team. The double team is very successful whenever two offensive men cross with one man dribbling the ball at the foul line extended or in the corner. It is true that we cross two offensive men on our weak-side series, but if you review the series, you will notice that this interchange is taking place about 15′ to 16′ away from the basket. We believe that an attempted double team in this area is not very effective because almost every time the double team fails, the offensive team has an easy shot. The distance that we maintain between our point man dribbling the ball and our wing man also aids in keeping the wing man's defensive man from doubling up on our point man whenever our point man reverses his dribble or is forced to turn his back and reverse it. In Figure 8-1, if 0-2's defensive man would attempt a steal from such a distance, 0-1 has plenty of time to give up the ball before X-2 gets near him.

Option 1 of the *Go Play* enables us to take advantage of an existing mismatch between our wing man and a shorter man defending against him.

We are convinced that the best place to have our wing man take advantage of such a mismatch is close to the basket. Every time a mismatch comes about, we want our bigger man to get the ball close to the basket where he can maneuver his smaller defender into affording him an easy shot or foul or, preferably, both, hoping it will result in a three-point play. The last thing we want our bigger man to do in such a situation is to shoot a 20′ or 25′ jump shot. We can always get a 20′ or 25′ jump shot. We don't have to have a mismatch in order to set up such a shot.

We impress upon our bigger boys that every time one of these shots is taken, the smaller defender is given four advantages unnecessarily. They are:

1. The advantage of a missed shot.
2. The advantage of keeping you away from the boards.

3. The advantage of not forcing him into committing a foul.
4. The advantage of forcing you into taking a poor percentage shot.

Without including in their offense the *Go Play* or a play designed for such situations, most coaches ask their bigger boys to drive on the smaller defender. This is a fine maneuver if the bigger boy is a good dribbler and a good driver. He has to be good because the smaller defender is usually quicker and a better defensive man against the dribble than the bigger boy is accustomed to. However, if he cannot dribble or drive well, such mismatches usually go for nought. We believe that even though the bigger boy may be a good driver, to have him dribble from a wing position to the basket is not as advantageous as it would be for us to have him gain possession of the ball from a pass near the basket. If he gains possession of the ball near the basket, he has the extra advantage of playing one-on-one with his man and yet having a live dribble available. If he were to dribble the ball to the low post, he would have to shoot a jump shot or lay-up off the dribble. The disadvantage comes when he is forced to pick up the dribble. Once he picks up the dribble in the low post, he doesn't have as many opportunities to score. The live dribble here is the important advantage. In our *Go Play* the bigger boy is afforded this advantage every time.

The philosophy behind the *Go Play* in regard to the mismatch is to get the ball to the bigger wing man in the low post. To insure his getting the ball, the proper execution of his pivot is essential. In Figure 8-1, wing man 0-2, after hearing the key, breaks with his back to 0-1 to the low post. Upon reaching the low post position, 0-2 should come to a jump stop with one foot in front of the other. If the front foot is the left foot, 0-2 pivots on both feet in a clockwise direction. Point man 0-1 should pass 0-2 the ball just as soon as he turns. If wing man 0-2 stops in the low post position with his right foot in advance of his left, 0-2 will pivot in a counter clockwise direction to receive his pass from 0-1.

In each case the pivots are made quickly and off the balls of both feet.

The *Go Play* is a play designed primarily to get the ball into our wing man. Throughout the years many of our best scorers have been wing men. I believe that this play made it much easier for those high-scoring wing men to score because it is designed to give them possession of the ball in floor positions that are ideal for shooting. The play gives the wing man four different opportunities to gain possession of the ball at four excellent floor positions (Figure 8-2).

We have previously discussed in detail the procedures used in getting the ball to a wing man positioned in floor position 1. We will now describe how we get the ball to our wing men in floor position 2 with a discussion of Option 2, a pass to the wing man in the high post position.

In Figure 8-3, 0-1 calls out "Go," and continues his dribble to the

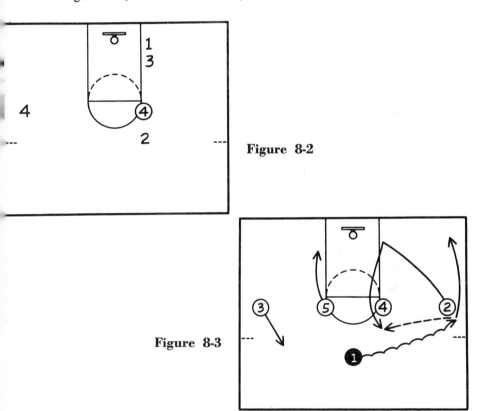

Figure 8-2

Figure 8-3

right wing position. 0-2 breaks to the low post position and pivots to receive a pass from 0-1. Failing to receive the pass, 0-2 breaks up behind 0-4 to the top of the key. 0-1 passes the ball to 0-2, then moves to the corner. 0-5 watches the play develop, then sinks to and rebounds the weak side. 0-3 takes two steps out and protects defensively.

In Figure 8-4, 0-2, after receiving a pass from 0-1, cannot shoot

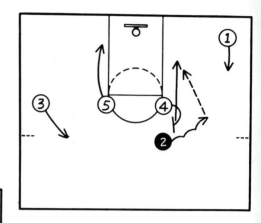

Figure 8-4

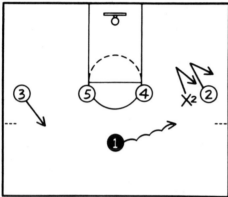

Figure 8-5

the ball. Pivotman 0-4 steps up to set a screen for wing man 0-2. 0-2 dribbles off 0-4's screen. 0-4 rolls to the basket. 0-2 will drive, shoot, or pass the ball to 0-4 rolling. 0-5 sinks to and rebounds the weak side. 0-3 takes two steps out and protects defensively against the fast break.

Once our point man decides to put the ball in play to a wing man, he must acknowledge his intentions by working the key. This key, as was previously discussed, is a dribble in the direction of the wing man. After the key is enacted, the wing man fakes down toward the basket, then breaks out quickly to try to receive a pass from point man 0-1 (Figure 8-5).

In this maneuver, point man 0-1 continues dribbling the ball as 0-2 is trying to free himself from defensive man X-2. Point man 0-1 doesn't stop his dribbling until he is ready to pass the ball off to a teammate. Here in Figure 8-5, the only reason he would not pass the ball to 0-2 would be the defensive position of his defensive man, X-2. To keep 0-2 from receiving a pass from 0-1, defensive man X-2 must position himself between 0-2 and the ball. If X-2 maintains this defensive position, 0-1 should not try to pass the ball off to 0-2 at the right wing position; instead, 0-1 should call out the word "Go," and immediately both the point man and the wing man move to enter into the *Go Play*. For wing man 0-2 to enter into this play, he must clear to the low post position.

Let's examine the defensive position of X-2 as 0-2 clears to the low post. Defensive man X-2 usually maintains the same inside position on 0-2 that he occupies in Figure 8-5. If he does, as 0-2 reaches the low post position, 0-2's baseline side is left unprotected (Figure 8-6). This being the case, if 0-1 can pass 0-2 the ball, 0-2 holds a tremendous offensive advantage over his defensive man. The pass into 0-2 must be made to him just as soon as he pivots. If there is a delay, it will give X-2 an opportunity to discourage a pass into 0-2 with his hands, or it will give X-2 an opportunity to move around in front of 0-2.

In analyzing the defensive options of defensive man X-2 defending against wing man 0-2 in the low post position, we find that X-2 can:

a. Play in front of 0-2 in the low post position.
b. Play to the inside of 0-2 with his right hand around in front of 0-2's body (Figure 8-6).

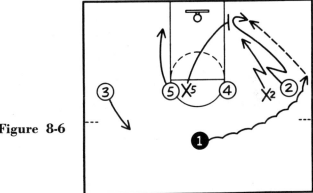

Figure 8-6

In both situations, point man 0-1 at the wing position should be able to get the ball to 0-2 most of the time. If 0-1 gets the ball into 0-2, 0-2 will work for the shot. When this situation arises, 0-2 can handle it with relative ease. Whenever 0-1 cannot pass the ball to 0-2 in the low post, 0-2 must move, clearing himself to the high post or top of the key to receive the ball.

If in Figure 8-6, 0-1 cannot pass the ball to 0-2 in the low post, then 0-2 will move to the high post or top of the key. He will make his move breaking out between 0-4 and 0-1, passing as close to 0-4 as possible in hopes of screening X-2 off on 0-4 (Figure 8-7).

If 0-2 is being defended in the low post by X-2 positioning himself between 0-2 and 0-1, 0-2 will move out to the high post by breaking out behind 0-4 in the hope that 0-4 can screen X-2 long enough for 0-2 to receive the ball from 0-1 (Figure 8-8). Whatever method 0-2 has to use to free himself, he eventually ends up at the high post position. In either case 0-1 can pass him the ball. Once 0-2 receives the ball near the top of the key, 0-4 will set a baseline screen for 0-2; then 0-4 will roll to the basket as was previously outlined in Option 2, the screen and roll for the wing man (Figure 8-4).

If in Figures 8-7 or 8-8, 0-1 cannot pass the ball to wing man 0-2 stationed at the top of the key, 0-2 will move to initiate Option 3 of the *Go Play,* a pass to the wing man in the second low post position (Figure 8-9).

In Figure 8-9, wing man 0-2 cuts from the top of the key to the low post, passing as close to 0-4 as possible in·the hope of clearing himself by rubbing his defensive man off on 0-4. If 0-2 is successful in clearing himself, point man 0-1 will pass him the ball. Wing man 0-2 must receive the ball as he cuts for the basket. If 0-2 does not receive the ball, he will clear to the off side, paving the way for pivotman 0-4 and point man 0-1 to enter into Option 4 of the *Go Play,* the drive off the pivot.

Here in Figure 8-10, 0-2 clears to the off side. 0-4 must become part of the play by screening for 0-1. 0-1 drives off the screen. 0-4 rolls to the basket. 0-1 shoots or passes to 0-4 rolling. 0-5 sinks to and rebounds the weak side; 0-3 takes two steps out and protects defensively.

If in Figure 8-10, 0-1 cannot shoot the ball or pass to 0-4 rolling, or if 0-2's defensive man does not clear to the off side with 0-2, 0-1 will enter into the weak-side series.

The weak-side series makes up Option 6 of the *Go Play.* Since the weak-side series has already been discussed it is not necessary to repeat it again.

Earlier we stated that once our point man starts to put the ball in play with a dribble, he should never stop dribbling until he is ready to pass the ball off to a teammate. If he picks the ball up voluntarily or if he is forced by his defensive man to pick the ball up, the effectiveness of our *Go Play* is severely curtailed. Experience has indicated that the three particular floor areas where this is most likely to occur are:

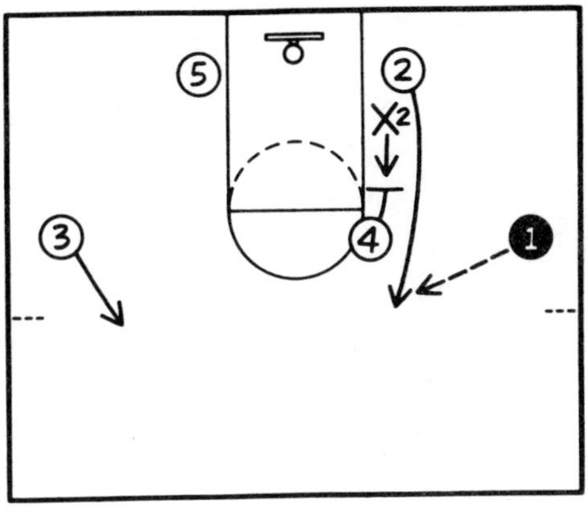

Figure 8-7

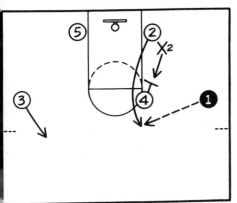

Figure 8-8

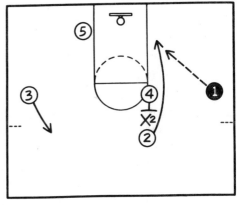

Figure 8-9

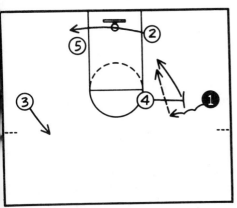

Figure 8-10

1. At the right wing position.
2. At the foul line area.
3. Out front at the top of the key.

Whenever our *Go Play* is stopped in these areas, to keep our offense operating effectively we rely upon our shuffle plays or our weak-side interchange series.

Although we can have difficulty in any of these three areas, statistics have shown that this play breaks down more often at the wing position than at any other place. When this occurs, we enter into the shuffle play as illustrated in Figures 8-11 and 8-12.

In Figure 8-11, 0-1 enacts the key for entering into the *Go Play* and dribbles to the wing position. 0-2 clears to the first low post position, moves to the top of the key and then down to the second low post position. If 0-1 is forced to pick up the ball, 0-2 does not clear to the off side. Wing man 0-3, realizing 0-1 has picked up his dribble, moves over to help out by making himself available for a pass. 0-5 sinks to and rebounds the off side.

Whenever 0-1 passes the ball out to 0-3, the pass-out acts as the key for our shuffle play (Figure 8-12). 0-5 will then break up from his rebounding position to receive a pass from 0-3. 0-3 dribbles over and passes to 0-5. 0-4 sets a screen for 0-1. 0-1, the first choice of 0-5, cuts off 0-4 and moves to the low post. As 0-1 cuts off 0-4, 0-3 cuts behind him, moving as close to 0-4 as possible, and forces his way down to the basket. As 0-3 cuts off 0-1, 0-4, the second choice of 0-5, breaks to the medium post towards the ball. As 0-4 cuts off 0-3, 0-2, the third choice of 0-5, breaks out to the top of the key. 0-5 can pass the ball to 0-1, 0-4, or 0-3. If he passes to 0-2, 0-2 can shoot or start the shuffle play on the other side with a pass to 0-3.

A question may arise here as to the play of wing man 0-2. At times in the execution of the *Go Play*, he is asked to clear to the off side. On other occasions 0-2 is asked to stay on the strong side of the court to help set up the shuffle. The question here is how does he know what function to perform. The explanation is simple; as long as point man 0-1 is dribbling the ball, wing man 0-2, after moving to the second low post position and failing to receive a pass from 0-1, will clear to the opposite side. If 0-1 is forced to pick up the ball, wing man 0-2 will stay on the strong side to act as an outlet man for point man 0-1, or to set up the shuffle. The point man dribbling the ball is the key to wing man 0-2's responsibilities. In Figure 8-10, after pivotman 0-4

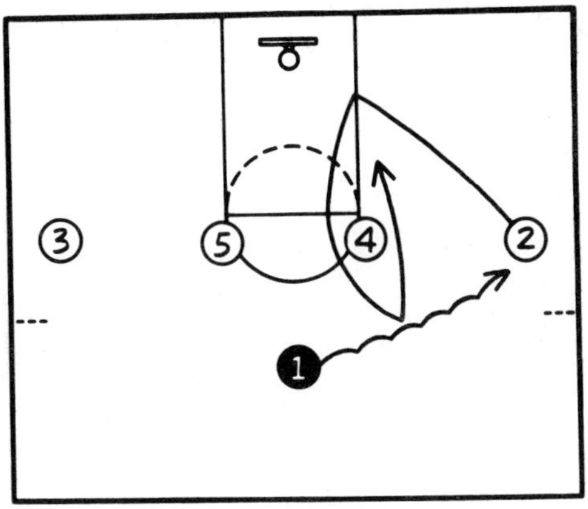

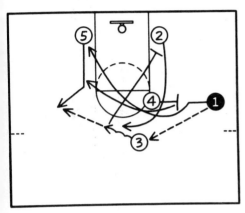

Figure 8-11

Figure 8-12

sets up the screen and roll, point man 0-1 is often forced to pick up his dribble in the foul area. If this occurs and 0-1 cannot pass to 0-4 rolling, it is 0-2's responsibility to get the ball from 0-1 (Figure 8-13).

The third and last area where our point man most frequently is forced to pick up his dribble occurs out front near the side of the circle.

In Figure 8-14, whenever point man 0-1 is forced to pick up the ball, 0-5, the off-side pivotman, is given the responsibility of providing a safety outlet for him. Further, point man 0-1 is instructed to look for the off-side pivotman every time he gets tied up with the ball. In such situations, after our point man passes the ball to the off-side pivotman, the play that his pass helps key is the shuffle. The shuffle play enacted here is the same as was previously outlined in Figure 8-12, except that the responsibilities of 0-3 and 0-5 have interchanged.

We have used this play on many occasions as a set play. We have used it at the start of a quarter or as the first play after a time-out. The play has been used to set up a shot for one of our outside shooting pivotmen, or to keep the defensive man guarding our pivotman from sagging. Finally, we have used the play against pressure defenses.

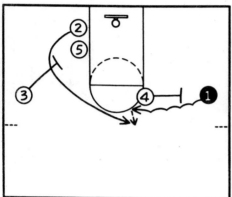

Figure 8-13

Figure 8-14

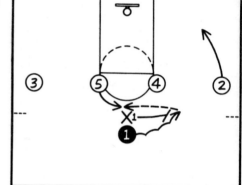

Considering the various uses of this option of the *Go Play* and of the other options described earlier, the full impact of the play's value should be clearly evident. I hope that I have made you realize that the dribble is a vital part of the 1-4 offense, and the *Go Play* is most certainly the one play our offense cannot do without.

9

PLAY 9:

THE DRIVE PLAY

Every team has its big play, one that the coach and his players believe is the bread and butter play of their offense. The 1-4 offense has as its big play Play 9, the *Drive Play*. The *Drive Play* is the play we go to whenever we need a basket, the play that our point man moves into most naturally, the play our players believe to be unstoppable. This play has brought more success than most of the others put together.

I am sure you realize that the success of a play depends entirely upon its execution. The best play ever derived from the game has little chance of success when it is improperly executed. Many times, however, good execution of even a poor or mediocre play brings surprisingly good results. Therefore, the only explanation we can offer to you to account for the success of the *Drive Play* is execution. We are able as a team to execute this play better and more often than any other play in our offense.

More than anything else, I believe, the *Drive Play* in our 1-4 offers a new approach to the game. This play, like so many others, is designed to create the mismatch by involving those players possessing the greatest height differentials. In our offense this means we try to cause a mismatch between the two defensive men defending against our pivotman and our point man. The play itself is not new, and I don't intend to mislead you into believing that it is a product of our own creativeness. It most certainly is not. However, in fairness to us, I am sure that there are not too many coaches in the country who have employed its use to the extent we do. We use it almost exclusively as a complete offense because of the play's simplicity of execution and the number of options it makes available for our use. There are eight

121

options to Play 9, the *Drive Play,* each of which will be discussed in depth as Chapter 9 unfolds.

OPTION 1: SCREEN AND ROLL, HIT THE PIVOT

In Figure 9-1, 0-4 moves out and sets a screen for 0-1, then rolls to the basket. 0-1 drives off the screen and passes to 0-4 rolling to the basket. 0-2 sinks to the baseline as soon as 0-4 moves out to screen. 0-5 sinks to and rebounds the off side. 0-3 takes two steps out to protect defensively.

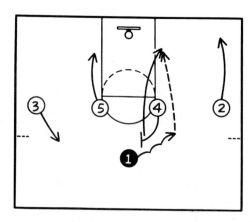

Figure 9-1

The success of Option 1 depends almost entirely upon the play of pivotman 0-4. His responsibilities in the play are to initiate the play, set the proper screen, force the switch on defense, make the proper roll, and shoot the ball if he receives it. These responsibilities are so important that we will examine each one independently and thoroughly.

Initiating the Play

With our point man bringing the ball down court, but after he crosses the mid-court jump-ball circle, both pivotmen break out from their baseline positions to their high post positions with hopes of gaining possession of the ball from 0-1. If point man 0-1 cannot pass the ball into one of the pivotmen, he will continue his dribbling in hopes of penetrating to a floor position as close to the top of the key as possible. As point man 0-1 is trying to dribble the ball to the top of the key, both pivotmen have already executed their jump stop and are standing stationary in their high post positions. With point man 0-1 near the top of the key and once it becomes evident to the pivotman closest to 0-1 that he is not going to receive a pass from 0-1, pivotman 0-4 moves out from his high post position to set a screen for 0-1. With such movement by 0-4, the *Drive Play* is keyed and its execution begins.

The Screen

At this point it is quite evident that the *Drive Play* really is an aftergrowth of Play 7, *Hit the Pivot*. It is only after our pivotman fails to get the ball from our point man that we execute the *Drive Play*. Our pivotmen are instructed to enter into this play every time they can, just as long as the point man is in the proper floor position. As the pivotman comes out to set the screen, we prefer to have both point man 0-1 and his defensive man standing in a stationary floor position. To accomplish this, point man 0-1 must have a method of freezing or controlling his defensive man. The method used for such purposes is the dribble. Since point man 0-1 is continually dribbling the ball, to freeze his defensive man he must change the rhythm of his dribble by increasing the force he applies to the ball and the number of dribbles per second. While doing this, he should constantly shift his weight from one foot to the other as rapidly as possible. Our point man must not only give his defensive man the impression that he is looking for a drive opportunity, but must take advantage of one if it ever comes about.

It is imperative that point man 0-1 wait until 0-4 takes a stationary position next to 0-1's defensive man. The position taken by 0-4 next to 0-2's defensive man should be one in which:

  a. He is as close to the defensive man as possible.
  b. His feet are shoulder width apart.
  c. His inside hand, the right one in this case, is carried on his right hip.
  d. He stands erect, positioning his body so that his head is in front of the defensive man's body rather than behind it.

Many times 0-1's defensive man will try to go over the top of 0-4's screen before 0-1 begins to drive off it. Point man 0-1 should anticipate such actions, and when they arise drive to his left after performing a cross-over dribble.

Forcing the Switch on Defense

Pivotman 0-4 must force a switch on defense to come about between his defensive man and the defensive man of 0-1. This can be accomplished mainly by 0-4's assuming the correct floor position next to 0-1's defensive man. With 0-4 in the desired position, the switch is inevitable and must come about after 0-1 drives off it and 0-4 rolls to the basket.

Point man 0-1 is also an important factor in influencing the switch on defense. Point man 0-1 must have patience, for without it he will begin his drive off 0-4 before 0-4 has assumed the desired stationary position. In doing so he can cause 0-4 to commit a foul by moving into 0-1's defensive man. Also without 0-4 in a stationary position, it is much easier for 0-1's defensive man to get around the screen and therefore make a switch on defense unnecessary.

The Proper Roll

Once 0-4 has set the desired screen for point man 0-1 and 0-1 drives off it, 0-4 rolls to the basket. The success of the play, naturally, is dependent upon the five functions that 0-4 must successfully perform, but the play usually breaks down more frequently when 0-4 is rolling toward the basket than at any other time.

In rolling to the basket, 0-4 must pivot on his right foot, turn in a counter-clockwise direction, and keep his eyes on 0-1 at all times. 0-4 starts his pivot after 0-1 starts the drive and after 0-4 makes contact with 0-1's defensive man. Once 0-4 makes contact with 0-1's defensive man, he should never lose this contact. 0-4 must try to force 0-1's defensive man to go behind 0-4 so that he cannot move into a position where he can possibly make an interception of a pass from 0-1. 0-4's most common error occurs when he allows 0-1's defensive man to slide between 0-4 and the ball. If 0-4 maintains contact on 0-1's defensive man, he can practically force the defensive man to stay behind him long enough for 0-1 to get the ball into 0-4.

Pivotman 0-4 must never make his roll to the basket too wide. We tell our pivotmen to use the free-throw lane lines as a guide when they roll as close as possible to the lane line on their side of the court (Figure 9-1).

Shooting the Ball

Once 0-4 receives a pass from 0-1 (Figure 9-1), shooting the ball is certainly important. This is probably the easiest function 0-4 must perform. In shooting the ball, there are only two significant points that 0-4 must be made aware of. *First,* whenever he shoots the ball he must make the shot or get fouled in the process of shooting. *Second,* since 0-1's defensive man is much smaller than 0-4, the only man on the floor who can successfully stop 0-4 from shooting is the defensive man of 0-5. Therefore, whenever 0-5 calls for the ball signifying he has been left open, 0-4 must forget about shooting and pass the ball to him. If pivotman 0-4 executes his responsibilities properly, we should end up scoring a basket, provided 0-1 can successfully perform his duties. The functions of 0-1 on the drive play, hit the pivotman rolling, are to:

1. Freeze or control his defensive man (previously discussed).
2. Display patience by waiting for 0-4 to set the proper screen (previously discussed).
3. Drive off the screen (previously discussed).
4. Keep his eyes glued on pivotman 0-4's defensive man.
5. Watch the left arm of 0-4's defensive man before attempting to pass the ball to 0-4 rolling.
6. Try to make quick, straight passes rather than a lob pass or a bounce pass.

As point man 0-1 drives off the screen set for him by pivotman 0-4, 0-1's eyes must be focused on 0-4's defensive man. 0-4's defensive man is the key from which point man 0-1 determines what play he will run. If after 0-1 drives off 0-4's screen, 0-4's defensive man switches, 0-1 should return the ball to 0-4 rolling to the basket (Option 1, Screen and roll and hit the pivot). Whenever the switch occurs, 0-1 must pass the ball to 0-4. It is 0-4's responsibility to get himself clear on the roll in the manner we discussed earlier. For 0-1 to pass the ball to 0-4, he must get the ball past the left arm of 0-4's defensive man who is now guarding 0-1. We want 0-1 to force the left arm of the defensive man downward so that a straight quick pass can be thrown past his ear. We ask our point man not to throw a lob pass to 0-4 rolling because we believe that 0-5's defensive man has an oppor-

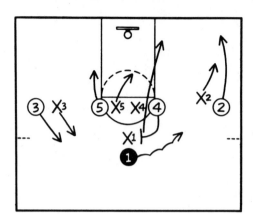

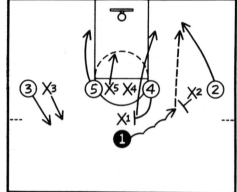

Figure 9-2

Figure 9-3

tunity to intercept it (Figure 9-2). We ask our point man to try to stay away from using a bounce pass as well, because we believe it to be too slow a pass and vulnerable to a possible interception by 0-1's defensive man guarding 0-4.

If both the point man 0-1 and the pivotman 0-4 execute their responsibilities properly, the play is unstoppable. Usually, however, if the play is run successfully against them a few times, the defense will make an adjustment. The possible adjustments that the defensive men in Figure 9-2 can make against Play 9, the *Drive Play* are:

1. Defensive man X-2 may try to shut off point man 0-1's drive and fail to pick up 0-2 in the corner.
2. Defensive man X-2 may try to double-team point man 0-1 as he drives off 0-4's screen.
3. Defensive man X-5 may sag to help X-1 defend against 0-4 rolling.
4. Defensive men X-4 and X-1 may not switch on defense.
5. Defensive men X-4 and X-1 may not switch on defense, and defensive X-2 may try to stop 0-1 from driving.

126

6. Defensive men X-4 and X-1 may not switch on defense, but X-4 may move out and employ a fake switch to try to influence 0-1 into picking up his dribble.
7. Defensive men X-4 and X-1 switch but do a good enough job defensively to keep 0-4 from getting the ball.

In analyzing the list of possible defensive adjustments, it is evident each one is capable of causing game problems for our Option 1, screen and roll, hit the pivot play. To cope adequately with such defensive adjustments, we're forced to counter with adjustments in our *Drive Play*. These adjustments in our offense are called options. All of the options we've made in our *Drive Play* and the defensive adjustments they are designed to meet will be described in detail.

OPTION 2: SCREEN AND ROLL, HIT THE WING MAN
CUTTING FOR THE BASKET

In Figure 9-3, 0-4 moves out to set a screen for 0-1; 0-2 sinks to the baseline; 0-1 drives off the screen; 0-4 rolls to the basket. If defensive man X-2 fails to pick up 0-2 as he sinks to the baseline, 0-2 will

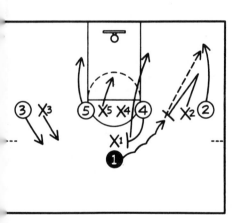

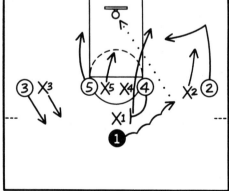

Figure 9-4

Figure 9-5

cut for the basket and 0-1 immediately passes him the ball for a shot. 0-5 sinks to and rebounds the off side. 0-3 takes two steps out and protects defensively.

OPTION 3: SCREEN AND ROLL, HIT THE WING MAN AT THE BASELINE

In Figure 9-4, 0-4 moves out to set a screen for 0-1. 0-2 sinks to the baseline. 0-1 drives off the screen. 0-4 rolls to the basket. If defensive man X-2 attempts to shut off 0-1's drive to the basket, 0-1 passes the ball to 0-2 at the baseline for a jump shot. 0-5 sinks to and rebounds the off side. 0-3 takes two steps out and protects defensively.

If defensive men X-4 and X-1 do not switch on defense, Options 4, 5, and 6 of the *Drive Play* are employed.

OPTION 4: SCREEN AND ROLL, TAKE THE SHOT

In Figure 9-5, 0-4 moves out to set the screen for 0-1. 0-2 sinks to the baseline, 0-1 drives off the screen and shoots the jump shot. 0-4

Figure 9-6

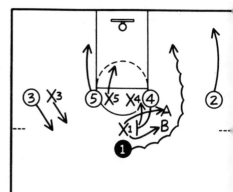

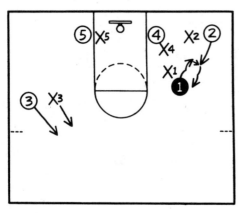

Figure 9-7

rolls to the basket and rebounds the shot. 0-5 sinks to and rebounds the off side. 0-3 takes two steps out and protects defensively.

The shot by 0-1 depends entirely on the play of defensive man X-1. Whenever 0-4 sets a screen on X-1, X-1 has two routes he can follow to get past the screen, Route A or Route B (Figure 9-6). If he decides to follow Route A, X-1 goes behind 0-4. Following such a route, X-1 has 0-4 between him and the man he is assigned to defend against, 0-1. With X-1 in such a position and X-4 defending against 0-4 rolling, 0-1 can easily shoot a jump shot without any interference from X-1.

OPTION 5: SCREEN AND ROLL, DRIVE
TO THE BASKET

If in Figure 9-6, defensive man X-1 selects to follow Route B after he has been screened by 0-4, he will provide 0-1 with a good drive opportunity. X-1 following such a route can't possibly beat 0-1 to the basket. If X-4 does not switch or if X-2 does not cut off his drive, 0-1 has an easy basket.

If 0-4 sets a poor screen or if 0-1, on his way to the basket, doesn't drive close enough to 0-4, X-1 will have ample room to follow Route B.

Under such circumstances X-1 can keep 0-1 from shooting the jump shot and at the same time keep 0-1 from driving to the basket as well. When this occurs, as it does many times during the course of a season, 0-1 must then play with wing man 0-2, who has taken a position near the baseline and sets up Option 6.

OPTION 6: SCREEN AND ROLL, HIT THE WING MAN
CROSSING

In Figure 9-7, 0-4, after rolling to the basket, takes a position in the low post. 0-1, unable to shoot, drive or pass the ball to 0-4 or 0-2, continues his drive and his dribble toward defensive man X-2. 0-2 waits at the baseline until 0-1 brings the ball to him then cuts behind 0-1. 0-1 hands the ball off to 0-2. 0-2 takes the hand-off and can shoot, pass to 0-4 under or play with 0-3 at the point. 0-5 rebounds the off side. 0-3 moves out to the point position and waits for 0-2 to start a play with him. If 0-2 shoots or passes to 0-4, 0-3 protects defensively. If 0-2 decides to play with 0-3, 0-2 dribbles toward him and hands the ball off in an interchange type action (Figure 9-8).

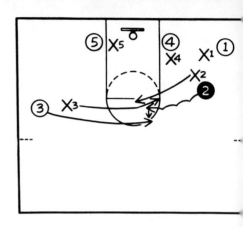

Figure 9-8

If 0-3 cannot shoot, pass to 0-4, or 0-1, he will continue the interchange movement with 0-1.

Whenever the defense does not employ the switch between the defensive man of 0-1 and of 0-4, most teams make 0-4's defensive man employ a fake switch type maneuver in hopes of influencing point man 0-1 into picking up his dribble. If the fake switch is successful, then 0-1's defensive man, regardless of how he's been screened, can easily catch up to 0-1 in time to keep him from shooting.

The fake switch is usually employed with 0-4's defensive man X-4 occupying a floor position next to 0-4's outside arm (Figure 9-9). As X-4 is assuming such a floor position, he will usually place his right hand in the small of 0-4's back. When 0-1 drives off the screen, X-4 will jump out in his path to try to get him to pick up his dribble, and at the same time he will keep his hand in 0-4's back so that the latter cannot roll to the basket.

To combat the fake switch, 0-1 and 0-4 must be alerted to its employment. It is the coach's responsibility to inform 0-1 and 0-4, as well as the rest of the team members, of such a development. Whenever a team employs the jump switch, they use it because they were coached into using it. They do not use it one time and not the next; they employ its use all the time or never. Our knowing this gives us a tremendous offensive advantage. When the offensive team knows how the defense is going to react to a play, they can make the necessary offensive adjustments to combat successfully any defense. The adjustments we make in our drive play to combat the fake switch are:

   a. We make our point man drive hard off the screen and go to the basket.

   b. We make 0-4 break to the basket just as soon as he feels X-4's hand in his back or just as soon as X-4 takes a position alongside him.

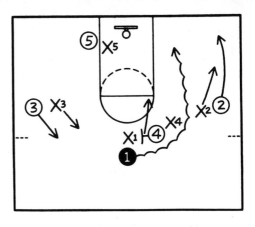

Figure 9-9

If our point man knows that the jump switch is to be employed by the defense, he will be expecting X-4 to jump out in the path of his dribble. If he is expecting such a maneuver, 0-1 is not taken by surprise when it happens. The surprise element in the jump switch is what makes it effective. Take it away and the jump switch can be more a detriment than an asset. Also, 0-1 must understand that it is a physical impossibility for X-4 to hold 0-4 with one hand and, at the same time, use the other hand to interfere with 0-1's dribble. With 0-1 fully aware of this impossibility and reassured by our insistence that a big man like X-4 is not capable of taking the ball away from a good little man like himself. 0-1 is equipped with the necessary confidence to make the play a success just by driving past X-4 to the basket.

The second method we employ to combat the jump fake switch involves the use of pivotman 0-4. In Figure 9-9, when 0-4 moves out to set a screen for point man 0-1, defensive man X-4 moves to the defensive position as illustrated. X-4 takes a floor position to the outside of 0-4, between 0-4 and the sideline. Let's analyze the defensive adjustments X-4 must make to end up in the floor position just described. When point man 0-1 first brings the ball down court, pivotman 0-4 stations himself close to the basket near the baseline. To keep 0-4 from receiving a pass near the basket, thus securing a lay-up shot, X-4 must station himself between 0-4 and the basket. Whenever 0-4 breaks out to the high post, X-4 must maintain this inside defensive position, otherwise 0-4 could receive a pass from 0-1 and secure an easy lay-up shot from a power right with his back to the basket. In order for X-4 to station himself in a floor position where he can administer the fake switch, he must move, as 0-4 moves out to screen for 0-1, from an inside defensive position on 0-4 to a defensive position on 0-4's outside (Figure 9-9). To combat the fake switch, 0-4 should break to the basket immediately after X-4 reaches this outside defensive position described. 0-4 should not concern himself with trying to

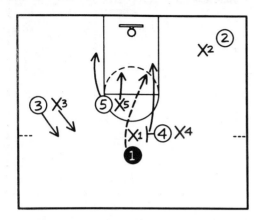

Figure 9-10

screen for 0-1, but should devote his attention solely to the selection of the best time to make his break to the basket. With X-4 occupying such a defensive position, he cannot protect against 0-4 breaking to the basket as illustrated in Figure 9-10.

OPTION 7: CONTAIN THE DEFENSIVE CENTER

Occasionally, even when there is a switch on defense between defensive man X-4 and defensive man X-1, point man 0-1, many times for a number of reasons, cannot immediately get the ball to 0-4 rolling to the basket. If 0-4 does not receive the ball from 0-1 as he is rolling to the basket, 0-4 must take his smaller defender to the low post position on the strong side of the court (Figure 9-11).

In this play, 0-4 moves out to set a screen on defensive man X-1. Defensive man X-4 takes a defensive position to the outside of 0-4. 0-2 sinks to the baseline. 0-1 drives off the screen. 0-4 rolls to the basket. X-1 switches on defense and picks up 0-1 as 0-1 drives off the screen. X-1 switches on defense and picks 0-4 as 0-4 rolls to the basket. 0-5 sinks to and rebounds the off side. 0-3 takes two steps out and protects defensively. Once 0-4 reaches the low post position, he must maneuver his smaller opponent into a defensive position, where

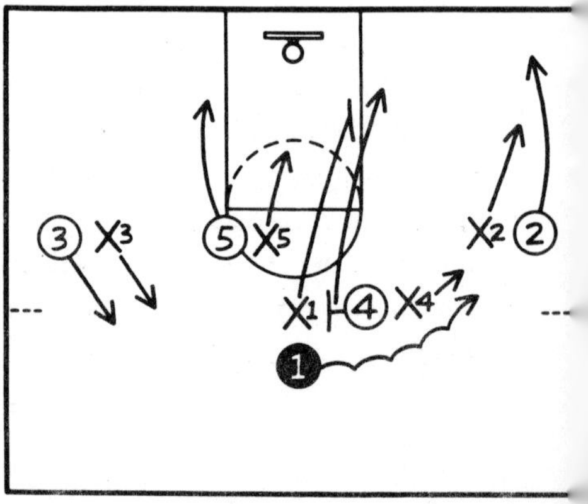

Figure 9-11

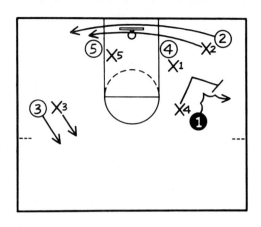

Figure 9-12

he cannot intercept or deflect a possible pass from 0-1. As 0-4 rolls to the low post, 0-1 is still dribbling the ball. In such a situation 0-1 is instructed to contain defensive man X-4 by dribbling the ball away from the basket and out toward the foul line extended (Figure 9-12). Once 0-2 realizes that 0-1 is containing X-4, 0-2 clears to the off side. With 0-2 clearing to the off side X-2 usually clears out with him. With both men clearing to the off side, 0-1 and 0-4 have half the court to maneuver in. If 0-4 can get himself clear, 0-1 will pass the ball into him and take advantage of the mismatch. If X-4 doesn't move all the way out to defend against 0-1, 0-1 will have a good percentage shot. We encourage 0-1 to take this shot if it presents itself for the two following reasons:

a. Point man 0-1 has a very good chance of scoring.
b. In the event 0-1 misses the shot, pivotman 0-4 has good rebounding position as well as a height advantage over X-1.

We believe the contain option to be a very strong offensive play. It offers many offensive advantages that you can make use of quickly and effectively. The play is so effective that the defensive team must make some sort of adjustment to try to stop it. The defensive adjustments that we expect teams to make and which we are prepared to combat are:

1. In Figure 9-13, defensive man X-5 will leave 0-5 unprotected and move over to help defend against 0-4.
2. In Figure 9-14, defensive man X-2 will not clear to the opposite side with 0-2, but will instead hold his position next to 0-4 to try to stop him from receiving a pass.

In Figure 9-13, if defensive X-5 leaves 0-5 unprotected and moves over to defend against 0-4, 0-5 breaks up to the high post position on the strong side. 0-1 passes to 0-5; 0-5 shoots the ball. 0-4 rebounds

133

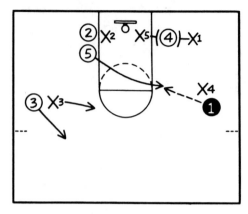

Figure 9-13

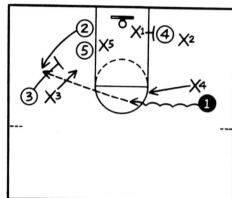

Figure 9-14

the strong side. 0-2 rebounds the weak side. 0-3 protects defensively against the fast break. If X-5 leaves 0-4 to stop 0-5 from shooting, 0-5 passes the ball to 0-4 under the basket.

The second defensive adjustment used against the contain option is illustrated in Figure 9-14. Once 0-1 realizes that X-2 failed to clear to the opposite side, he immediately enters into Option 8.

OPTION 8: THE WEAK-SIDE SERIES

In Figure 9-14, 0-1 after realizing that defensive man X-2 has failed to clear to the opposite side, dribbles across the foul area keying the weak-side series. 0-3 sees the key and screens down for 0-2. 0-2 breaks out to the foul area. 0-1 passes to 0-2. 0-2 shoots the ball. 0-5 rebounds the strong side. 0-4 rebounds the weak side.

With the presentation of Figure 9-14, we have concluded our discussion of the *Drive Play* and the new approach it lends to the game. I hope that the simplicity of the play does not mislead you into thinking that its execution can be neglected or that a play that simple just can't be effective. I can honestly assure you that it has been our big play in the past and will continue to be the bread and butter play of our 1-4 offense as long as coaches continue to employ the types of defenses and the defensive thinking against us that are dominating our game today.

10

DEVELOPMENT OF THE

1-4 ZONE OFFENSE

Earlier we acknowledged that our 1-4 offense was developed as an outgrowth of an accident. We admitted that our defense was unable to cope with it and, consequently, we incorporated the 1-4 alignment into our regular zone offense. Our reasoning in taking such a step had been based on the assumption that since our own match-up zone defense had difficulty stopping the 1-4, it would be equally difficult for our opponents to contend with.

Armed only with such reasoning, we plunged right in and started to develop the offense we are using today. Our offense was really developed from the 1-3-1 zone offense that we were using at the time. We employed the use of the overload concept with our baseline man moving from corner to corner. Our 1-3-1 was based upon movement of our players, crisp passing, offensive rebounding, minimal dribbling, and good outside shooting. Naturally you will find that many of these concepts have been incorporated in the 1-4 as well. The 1-4 offense, like the 1-3-1 offense, is based upon the overload principle and philosophy. Although they are similar in this respect, it is also true that they differ most radically in their approaches to such concepts. The 1-3-1 zone offense we employed was based upon the overload concept of attacking the defense from the sideline areas of the court.

The 1-4 is also based upon the overload concept, but instead of overloading near the sideline areas, the overload is established across the middle of the court from foul line extended to foul line extended.

The Alignment Against the 2-3 Zone Defense

In Figure 10-1, three defensive men, X-4, X-5, and X-3 are trying to defend against four offensive men, 0-3, 0-5, 0-4, and 0-2.

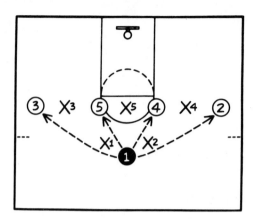

Figure 10-1

The Alignment Against the 1-2-2 Zone Defense

In Figure 10-2, defensive men X-3 and X-2 are at a disadvantage because there are two offensive players in their area instead of the usual one. Defensive man X-3 must try to keep 0-1 from passing the ball into 0-3 or 0-5. Defensive man X-2 must try to keep 0-1 from passing the ball into 0-4 or 0-2. Consider both situations; the result is that the two defensive men are outnumbered by the four offensive men.

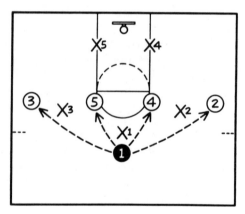

Figure 10-2

Figure 10-3

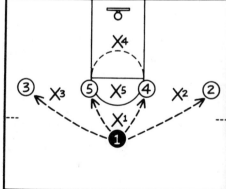

The Alignment Against the 1-3-1 Zone Defense

In Figure 10-3, three defensive men, X-3, X-5, and X-2 are trying to defend against four offensive men, 0-3, 0-5, 0-4, and 0-2.

It is evident from the illustrations that the 1-4 alignment invokes our overload against the three most common zone defenses in use today. With the overload acting as a base, we begin to develop our zone offense in the exact manner as we did our man-to-man offense. All of the rules governing our man-to-man offense apply here in the development of the zone offense as well.

It must be remembered that we are advocates of a controlled free-lance type of offense. We want to trigger the controlled part of our offense by means of a free-lance move. This free-lance move could be one that the point man has selected to use or it could be one that the defense has forced our point man to use. Whatever the case, point man 0-1 has the necessary freedom to attack the defense in whatever maneuver it makes necessary. He is armed with a means by which he can quickly force the defense to make a mistake and then carry out the correct movement to capitalize upon it. He must not have any pre-conceived thoughts as to what this movement should be, but must let the defense dictate his action. He must never become mechanical or stereotyped. His actions must be spontaneous, governed only by the defense and adhering to the primary objectives of our 1-4 offense designed especially for attacking zone defenses. The primary objectives of our 1-4 offense against any type of zone defense are:

1. To penetrate the defense by a pass or drive.
2. To force our defensive man into defending against two offensive men near the basket.
3. To isolate the defense to create one-on-one situations.
4. To have good offensive rebounding on all shots taken away from the basket.
5. To run our offense to the advantage side of the defense.
6. To force their good offensive men into playing defense as many times as possible.
7. To force the zone defensive players into playing man-to-man.

In the discussion that follows our remarks will be limited to the free-lance part of our offense. We will discuss the controlled phase of our offense in the chapter that follows. We again develop our 1-4 offense by means of a pass. Point man 0-1, in Figures 10-1, 10-2, and 10-3 has the opportunity to pass the ball to 0-3, 0-5, 0-4, or 0-2. Let's explore the possibilities afforded point man 0-1 on a pass to wing man 0-2, at which point he can:

a. Cut to the inside of pivotman 0-4 and go to the corner on the same side of the ball.
b. Cut to the outside of 0-4 and go to the opposite side of the court away from the ball.
c. Screen towards the ball by going behind 0-2.
d. Screen away from the ball for wing man 0-3.
e. Remain at the point position.
f. Screen toward the ball by going inside 0-2.
g. Screen away from the ball for 0-5.
h. Screen away from the ball for 0-4.

Point man 0-1 has exhausted all the opportunities afforded him on a pass to wing man 0-2. In analyzing the actions of point man 0-1 just described, I am sure that you will agree that there isn't anything more 0-1 can do after passing the ball to 0-2 that would be constructive in nature. In fact, we believe that we've gone too far in presenting the movements of 0-1, especially f, g, and h. We're of the opinion these actions are of little or no value and consequently we ask 0-1 not to pursue them. We ask you to be aware of the possibility of such courses of action but, after due consideration to disregard them.

A PASS INTO THE PIVOT

Point man 0-1 can pass the ball into the pivot. Once he does he can:

1. Cut off the pivotman receiving the pass.
2. Screen away for wing man 0-3.
3. Screen away for pivotman 0-5.

Point man 0-1, after passing the ball to pivotman 0-4, could possibly screen for wing man 0-2. In our offense, however, we have a rule for wing men which requires them to break to the basket and clear to the opposite side each time the on-side center receives a pass. Consequently, in our system, on such a play it would be impossible for 0-1 to screen for 0-2. The screening game of 0-1 has been exhausted; therefore, we will move into the development of our 1-4 offense with the dribble.

THE DEVELOPMENT OF THE OFFENSE FROM A DRIBBLE

The dribble's importance in our zone attack is as important here as it was on our man-to-man offense. An adjustment must be made in the way its use influences the action of our wing men and our pivotmen. These adjustments will be discussed later in the chapter. The one thing that must be clearly understood in regard to the use of the dribble is that it is employed to get the ball to the wing. Whenever our point man wants to get the ball to the wing, he just dribbles over to the wing position. Our wing man, upon realizing that the point man is dribbling the ball over to the wing, will clear to the corner (Figure 10-4).

THE DEVELOPMENT OF THE OFFENSE BY MEANS OF A DRIVE

Discounting offensive rebounding, the drive to the basket is more important to the success of the 1-4 offense than any other single component from which the 1-4 is composed. We believe in the concept that good zone defenses can be beaten only by offensive teams that continually try to penetrate it. In attempting to penetrate a zone defense, there are only two methods we can employ: we can penetrate it by means of a pass or by means of a drive. Most coaches agree that the pass is a good method of penetrating a zone and consequently encourage each one of their players to employ its use. We, too, encourage our players to employ the pass, but we insist that each learn how to penetrate the defense by means of a drive as well. This really means that we encourage our pivotmen and our wing men, as well as our point men, to drive to the basket whenever they can.

To employ the use of the drive successfully against zone defenses, our players rely upon the use of the various one-on-one power moves

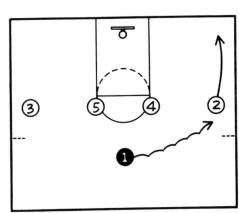

Figure 10-4

each must possess. These power moves are used exclusively whenever a driver is being guarded closely by a defensive man who has positioned himself between the driver and the basket. Most zone defensive teams position their defensive personnel in this manner. Thus, the power moves are ideal weapons for such close quarter play and deserve much of the credit for the success that our 1-4 offense has enjoyed. As was true in the development of our man-to-man offense, the drive in the zone offense takes precedence over any play pattern that has been entered into. Consequently, all team members must constantly anticipate drives to the basket by a teammate in possession of the ball.

If point man 0-1 has possession of the ball, he has three drive opportunities (Figure 10-5).

If point man 0-1 decides to pursue driving Route A, his teammates must view the drive in the same light as they would a fast break. Both pivotmen, after becoming aware of point man 0-1's driving route, will break to the basket (Figure 10-6).

In this situation, point man 0-1 may have an opportunity to drive all the way to the basket for a lay-up. Most of the time, however, 0-1 passes the ball to 0-5 or 0-4 as they are breaking to the basket.

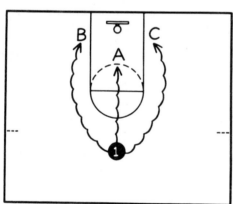

Figure 10-5

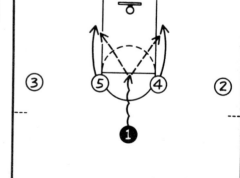

Figure 10-6

Let's consider the drive up the middle against the following three most common zone defenses: The 1-3-1, the 2-3, and the 1-2-2.

THE 1-3-1 ZONE DEFENSE

Figure 10-7 illustrates the drive up the middle against the 1-3-1 zone defense. Here point man 0-1 drives by defensive man X-1 and dribbles up the middle. Pivotmen 0-4 and 0-5 break to the basket. 0-2 sinks toward the corner. 0-3 begins to move out toward the point. 0-1 can pass the ball to 0-4 or 0-5 depending upon the play of defensive men X-5 and X-4.

In Figure 10-7 defensive men X-5 and X-4 are stationed in a tandem set, which is the same set that most coaches teach their defensive men to occupy when they have two defensive men defending against a three-man fast break. Consequently, point man 0-1 will handle this drive in the same manner as he does whenever he is the middle man on the fast break. His job is to penetrate toward the basket, getting as close to X-5 as possible, then trying to fake X-4 out of position so that a pass can be made to whichever pivotman is left unguarded.

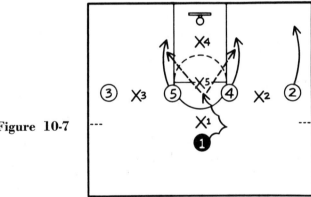

Figure 10-7

THE 2-3 ZONE DEFENSE

In Figure 10-8, point man 0-1 is successful in getting free of defensive men X-1 and X-2. When this occurs, pivotmen 0-5 and 0-4 break toward the basket. Point man 0-1 drives right at defensive man X-5. If defensive man X-5 selects to challenge 0-1, 0-1 passes the ball to 0-5 or 0-4. As pivotman 0-5 breaks to the basket, he concerns himself only with staying in front of defensive men X-3. Defensive man X-3 is

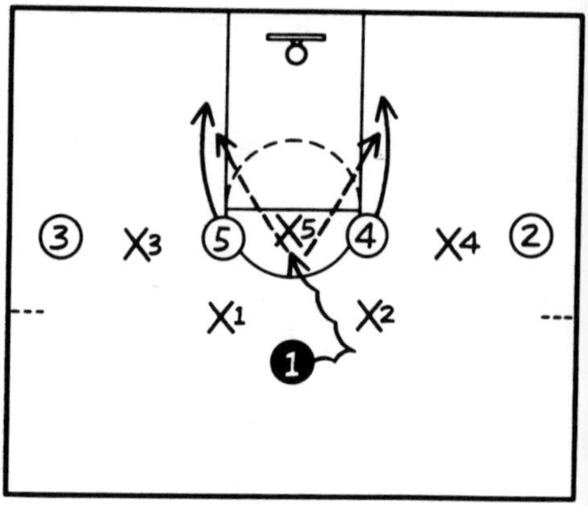

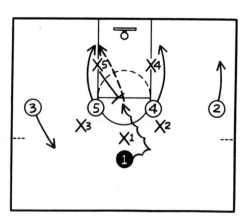

Figure 10-8

Figure 10-9

the only man who can possibly stop 0-5. The same is true of pivotman 0-4 and defensive man X-4. If, however, X-5 decides not to challenge 0-1, 0-1 can shoot the short jumper.

THE 1-2-2 ZONE DEFENSE

In Figure 10-9, point man 0-1 is successful in getting free of defensive man X-1. Pivotmen 0-5 and 0-4 break to the basket just as soon as they realize 0-1 is driving up the middle. Point man 0-1 should drive squarely to defensive man X-5. Whenever X-5 picks up 0-1, 0-1 should pass the ball to 0-5 under the basket. Driving Routes B and C in Figure 10-5 will be discussed later in Chapter 11 in Play 5, whenever the *Drive Off the Pivot* is presented.

Whenever wing man 0-2 gains possession of the ball, he has his choice of two drive opportunities (Figure 10-10). He can drive to his right and follow driving Route A to the basket, or he can select to drive to his left, reversing his dribble at the foul line and ending up at B. These two driving opportunities will be discussed later in Chapter 11, when Play 6, *the Wing Man Drives,* is presented.

Whenever pivotman 0-4 gains possession of the ball, he has the two drive opportunities illustrated in Figure 10-11.

The driving routes of 0-4 will be discussed in Chapter 11 when Play 4, *Hit the Pivot,* is presented.

In the development of the 1-4 offense from a shot, our offensive rebounding is the most important component to be considered. The emphasis of good offensive rebounding has been stressed once before in the earlier chapters of this book dealing with the development of our man-to-man offense.

Here in the zone offense, due to the increased number of outside shots that are available, offensive rebounding is even more essential than it is in our man-to-man. All of our plays then are developed from an offensive rebounding point of view. Our rebounding, whenever a shot is taken from the point, wing, and pivot positions, must be effective and consistent. Its effectiveness is determined by good rebounding positioning by our players and their ability in anticipating when a shot is to be taken. Its consistency comes about through constant practice and the continuous stressing of its importance to our players.

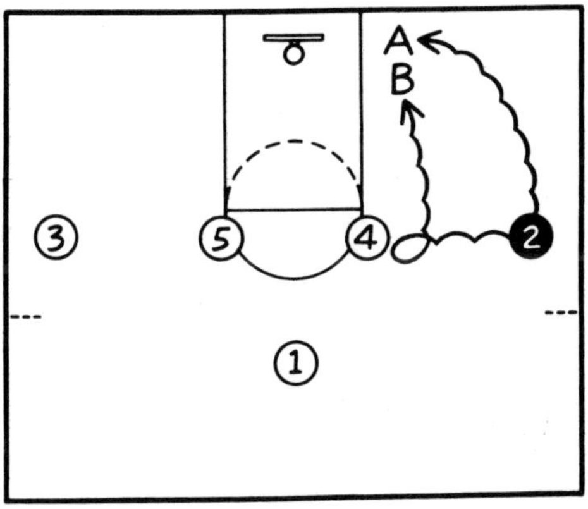

Figure 10-10

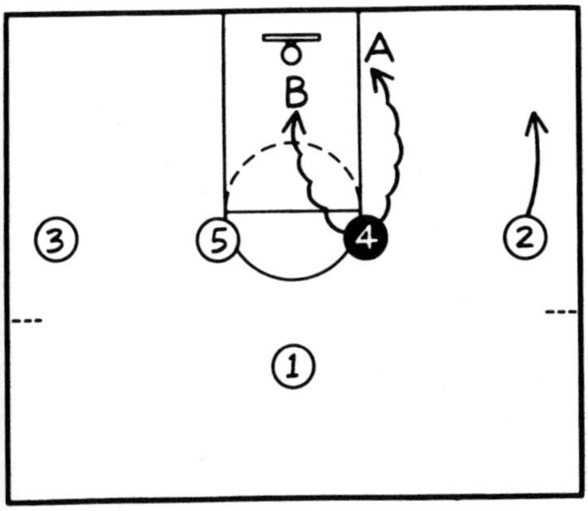

Figure 10-11

Figure 10-12 illustrates the offensive and defensive floor balance procedures after a shot is taken by point man 0-1. Here, whenever 0-1 shoots the ball from the right side of the top of the key, 0-2 moves towards the corner, and then has middle rebound responsibility. 0-4 rebounds the strong side. 0-5 rebounds the off side. 0-1 rebounds the foul area and becomes what we classify as a half rebounder. 0-3 takes two steps out to protect defensively. If a shot was taken by 0-2 at the wing position or by 0-1 from the right corner position, the rebounding and defensive floor balance positions would be identical to Figure 10-12. If a shot is taken by pivotman 0-4 (Figure 10-13), 0-4 rebounds his shot. 0-2 rebounds the strong side. 0-5 rebounds the off side. 0-1 rebounds the foul area as a half rebounder. 0-3 takes two steps out and protects defensively.

The offensive rebounding and the defensive floor balance positions outlined here have been drawn up for shots originating from the right side of the court. For shots taken from the left side, the rebounding and defensive floor balance positions for the players involved are reversed. The responsibilities of pivotmen 0-5 and 0-4 are reversed as is true of the responsibilities of wingmen 0-3 and 0-2.

Determining the Advantage Side

In the presentation of the overload concept of our 1-4 offense against the 1-2-2, 2-3, and 1-3-1 zone defenses, we were quick to point out that all the defenses are at a disadvantage when they are used against our 1-4. The defensive team is at a disadvantage whenever one of their defensive men is forced to defend against two offensive men in the same area. We know it is to our advantage to put the ball in play on the side of the court where one man is attempting to defend against two, so we designate the side of the court where this situation exists as the advantage side. We impress upon our point man that it is imperative for him to know the advantage side each time he brings the ball down court. Let's investigate the various zone defenses against our 1-4 alignment for purposes of determining just where the advantage side exists.

The 2-3 Zone

When confronted with our 1-4 offense, most of the 2-3 zone defensive teams we have faced have made some sort of adjustment in their

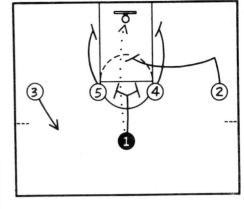

Figure 10-12

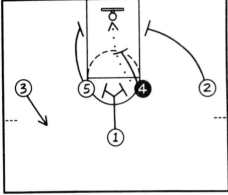

Figure 10-13

defense to try to shut off a pass from our point man into our pivotmen. Our advantage side is determined by their adjustments. If the defense fails to make this adjustment, we have our point man get the ball to one of the pivotmen until an adjustment is made.

Figure 10-14 illustrates the advantage right. Here defensive man X-4 is attempting to defend against pivotman 0-4 and wingman 0-2. Since defensive man X-4 is defending against two offensive men, he keys the advantage side to be to point man 0-1's right.

In Figure 10-15, defensive man X-3 is attempting to defend against pivotman 0-5 and wing man 0-3. Since defensive man X-3 is defending against two offensive men, he keys the advantage side to be point man 0-1's left.

Figure 10-16 illustrates the absence of an advantage side. Here, X-1 shifts out of his normal 2-3 zone defensive position to pick up wing 0-3. In doing so he permits X-3 to cover pivotman 0-5. In such cases the defense is picking up the offense man-to-man.

It is apparent that such a defensive alignment fails to establish an advantage side for the offensive team. What it does, however, is give us the benefit of playing against a man-to-man offense rather than a zone.

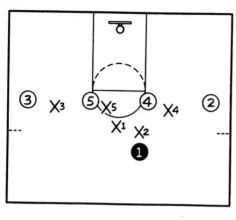

Figure 10-14

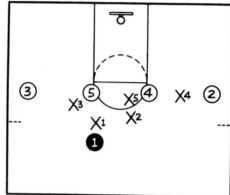

Figure 10-15

Figure 10-16

The 1-2-2 Zone

Figures 10-17 through 10-20 illustrate the advantage sides developed from adjustments made in the 1-2-2 zone defense.

Figure 10-17 illustrates the advantage right. Here defensive man X-2 is attempting to defend against pivotman 0-4 and wing man 0-2. Since defensive man X-2 is attempting to defend against two offensive men, he keys the advantage side to be to point man 0-1's right.

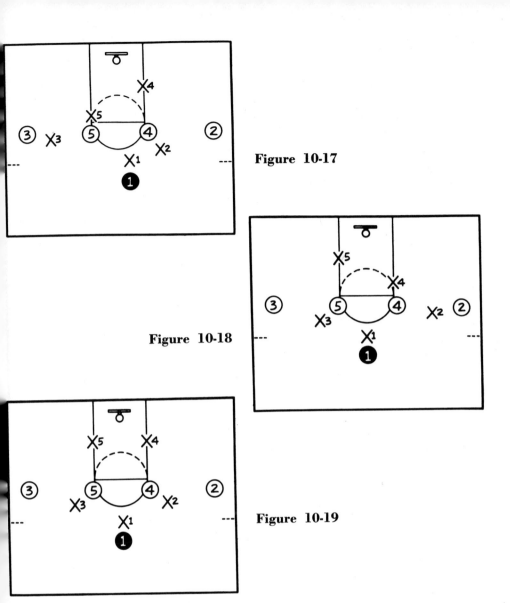

Figure 10-17

Figure 10-18

Figure 10-19

In Figure 10-18, defensive man X-3 is attempting to defend against pivotman 0-5 and wing man 0-3. Since defensive man X-3 is defending against two offensive men, he keys the advantage side to be to point man 0-1's left.

Figure 10-19 illustrates the advantage on both sides. Here both defensive men X-2 and X-3 are attempting to defend against two offensive men. Defensive man X-2 is attempting to defend against 0-4 and 0-2. Defensive man X-3 is attempting to defend against 0-5 and 0-2. In such cases the offense has an advantage on both sides.

Figure 10-20 illustrates the absence of an advantage side.

Here defensive men X-5 and X-4 have shifted out of their normal 1-2-2 zone defensive positions to pick up pivotmen 0-5 and 0-4. This permits defensive man X-3 to pick up 0-3 and defensive man X-2 to pick up 0-2. In such cases our offensive advantage side fails to materialize. What has developed, however, is that the defense is forced to play man-to-man instead of their normal zone.

The 1-3-1 Zone

Figures 10-21 through 10-23 illustrate the offensive advantage sides developed from adjustments made in 1-3-1 zone defenses.

In Figure 10-21, defensive man X-2 is attempting to defend against pivotman 0-4 and wing man 0-2. Since defensive man X-2 is attempting to defend against two offensive men, he keys the advantage side to be to point man 0-1's right.

In Figure 10-22, defensive man X-3 is attempting to defend against pivotman 0-5 and wing man 0-3. Since defensive man X-3 is defending against two offensive men, he keys the advantage side to be to point man 0-1's left.

In Figure 10-23, defensive men X-5 and X-4 have shifted out of their normal 1-3-1 zone defensive positions to pick up pivotmen 0-5

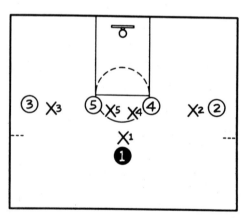

Figure 10-20

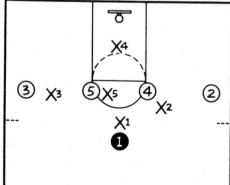

Figure 10-21

and 0-4. Defensive man X-3 picks up 0-3, and X-2 picks up 0-2. In such situations there is no advantage side. However, because of the realignment of the defensive players, the defense is now a man-to-man defense instead of a 1-3-1 zone. We have on many occasions referred to our 1-4 offense as being the modern offense for attacking all defenses. Earlier we explained our need and desire for one offense to be used against all defenses. Yet we seem to be contradicting ourselves as we constantly imply that our 1-4 is composed of two separate offenses, a 1-4 man-to-man offense and a 1-4 zone offense. We even went so far as to develop them separately. If we continue making our presentation along these lines, we will have two separate offenses, and our original goal of developing a multiple offense for use against all defenses will never be accomplished. I believe the time has come for us to develop the necessary ties between what we have presented as a man-to-man offense and our zone offense so that they can be one.

In reviewing our presentation of our man-to-man offense, we find that it consists of the following nine plays:

Play 1: *Pass and Cut, Clear to the Opposite Side.*
Play 2: *Pass and Cut, Go to the Corner.*
Play 3: *Pass and Screen Inside Toward the Ball* (*the Inside Screen*).

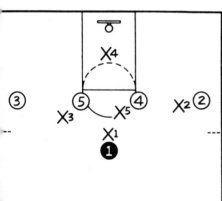

Figure 10-22

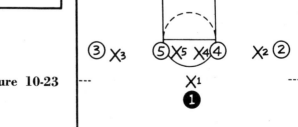

Figure 10-23

Play 4: *Pass and Screen Outside Toward the Ball (the Go-Behind).*

Play 5: *Pass and Screen Away from the Ball for the Off-Side Wing Man.*

Play 6: *Pass and Screen Away from the Ball for the Off-Side Pivot-man.*

Play 7: *Hit the Pivot.*

Play 8: *The Go Play.*

Play 9: *The Drive Play.*

Each play, as you recall, was developed from a free-lance move. The free-lance move keys or triggers the play the point man wants to run. We want each play to be triggered in this manner so that the defense never maneuvers us into a position where we cannot get our offense started. Some of the plays are not as good as others. We were honest and truthful in presenting both the strong and weak points of each.

Plays 3, 5, and 6 are of little value against zone defensive teams, so against zone defenses we stay away from using them as much as possible. If we delete these plays from our zone attack, our zone offense will consist of the remaining six plays. We refer to these six plays as the basic six. The tie-in between what we call our 1-4 man-to-man offense and our 1-4 zone offense is the basic six. In both offenses each play in the basic six is initiated in the same manner, a free-lance move. However, even though they are initiated in the same manner, they will differ greatly in the options they render. The basic six will be drawn up and discussed in detail against the 2-3, 1-3-1, and 1-2-2 zone defenses in Chapters 11, 12, and 13.

This concludes our discussion of the development of our zone offense. With our basic six we will present the controlled plays of our zone offense and show how effective they can be against the zone defenses we encounter.

11

THE BASIC SIX

AGAINST THE 2-3 ZONE DEFENSE

The basic six, when taken collectively, have proven to be very successful against 2-3 zone defense. When the plays are scrutinized separately, some prove to have been more successful than others. If we were to chart the six plays, and place each in the proper category according to their effectiveness against the 2-3 zone, the chart would consist of the following three categories:

   a. Those plays in the basic six that we consider bad plays.
   b. Those plays in the basic six that we consider mediocre plays.
   c. Those plays in the basic six that we consider superior plays.

With these three categories in mind, a chart could be constructed in the following manner:

TYPE DEFENSE: 2-3 ZONE		TYPE OFFENSE: 1-4 ZONE
Bad Plays	*Mediocre Plays*	*Superior Plays*
None	1. Play 1: Pass and Cut, Clear to the Opposite Side.	1. Play 2: Pass and Cut, Go to the Corner.
	2. Play 5: The Go Plays or Dribble Over.	2. Play 3: Pass and Go Behind.
		3. Play 4: Hit the Pivot.
		4. Play 6: The Drive Play.

151

From the chart then, we have four plays in the basic six that we believe to be superior against a 2-3 zone defense. Consequently, if our scouting reports indicate that our next opponent has been using a 2-3 zone defense, we would naturally run these four superior plays in our practice sessions, emphasizing their importance and proper execution. We should mention here, however, that we would not think of neglecting the other two plays since our opponents might use another defense where their use would be necessary.

PLAY 1: PASS AND CUT, CLEAR TO THE OPPOSITE SIDE

According to our chart, Play 1, or the *Opposite Side Play,* is listed as a mediocre play. We will discuss this play in detail so that it can be clearly understood why it is just a mediocre play.

Before point man 0-1 can intiate the execution of Play 1, he must first bring the ball down court and put it in play to a wing man. He has the option of passing the ball to either of our two wing men, 0-2 or 0-3. If Play 1 is to have even a slight chance of working, point man 0-1 must first of all pass the ball to the wing man on the side of the court where the offensive team does not have the advantage (Figure 11-1).

Here point man 0-1 passes the ball to wing man 0-2 on the strong side. If 0-1 were to pass the ball to 0-3 on the advantage side, 0-3 would probably drive to the basket, shoot, or pass the ball to 0-5, and Play 1 would never even get started. This partly accounts for Play 1's mediocrity. In the execution of our opposite play, the play of pivotmen 0-4 and 0-5 against zone defenses must be explained.

As you recall, our on-side pivotman in our man-to-man offense had

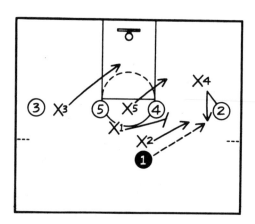

Figure 11-1

one assignment on every play. His assignment, which was to become part of the play being executed, he carried out by:

1. Cutting for the basket after a pass into the wing man.
2. Screening toward the ball after a pass into the wing man.
3. Screening away from the ball for the off-side pivotman, after a pass into the wing man.

Here in our zone offense, the on-side pivotman again is asked to become part of the play. He must understand, however, that screening toward the ball on the side of the court where our plays are first initiated is usually of little value. Consequently, against zone defenses we discourage the screen toward the ball. Instead, we prefer to have the on-side pivotman remain in the pivot in hopes that his presence there will isolate the defensive pivotman. Therefore, our on-side pivotman, after a pass to the wing man, can become part of the play by:

1. Cutting for the basket.
2. Screening away from the ball for the off-side pivotman.
3. Remaining in the pivot and letting the play develop.

Our off-side pivotman's assignment, after a pass to the wing man on the opposite side of the court, could be:

a. To sink to and rebound the off side.
b. To play with the on-side pivotman.
   1. If he sets a screen, break toward the ball.
   2. If he cuts to the basket, break toward the ball.
c. To cut from the high post on the off side to the low post on the strong side.

In Play 1, *Pass and Cut, Clear to the Opposite Side,* we prefer to have our on-side pivotman remain stationary and our off-side pivotman sink to and rebound the off side. However, if our on-side pivotman cuts for the basket or screens for the off-side pivotman, the play can still be effective, but probably will not reach its conclusion on the off side. Before we explain what we mean by the play reaching its conclusion on the off side, we must first diagram Option 1.

Option 1 of Play: Hit the Cutter

In Figure 11-2, 0-1 passes the ball to 0-2 and then cuts to the basket. 0-2 passes to 0-1 for a shot. 0-5 sinks to and rebounds the off side. 0-4 rebounds the strong side. 0-3 breaks out to the top of the key.

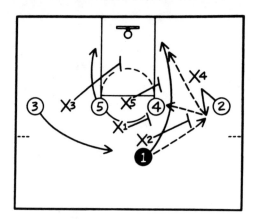

Figure 11-2

Option 2 of Play 1: Hit the Pivot

Figure 11-2 also illustrates pivotman 0-4 isolating pivotman X-5 to such an extent that it is impossible for him to cover 0-4 and 0-1 at the same time. If X-5 picks up point man 0-1, 0-2's second option is to pass the ball to pivotman 0-4.

If 0-2 cannot pass the ball to 0-1, his first choice, or 0-2, his second choice, he passes the ball out to the top of the key to wing man 0-3 (Figure 11-3).

> ZONE RULE 1: Wing men, after passing the ball, cut to the basket, or they can move away from the direction of the ball.

> ZONE RULE 2: Point man, after receiving a pass at the top of the key from a wing man, puts the ball in play on the opposite side of the court (Figure 11-3).

In Figure 11-3, 0-2 passes the ball out to the top of the key to 0-3, then, adhering to Zone Rule 1, cuts to the basket. 0-1 breaks out to receive a pass from 0-3. 0-3 passes to 0-1, initiating the off-side series. 0-1 can shoot or pass to 0-2, 0-5, or 0-3.

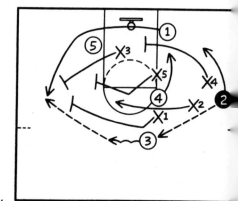

Figure 11-3

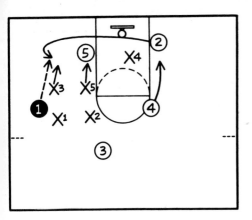

Figure 11-4

If point man 0-1 cannot shoot the ball, he must first look to pass the ball to 0-2 close to 0-5.

In Figure 11-4, if 0-1 passes the ball to 0-2, 0-2 should have the shot. If 0-2 is not clear enough to get a shot, 0-1 should not throw him the ball. If 0-1 does not throw 0-2 the ball, 0-2 moves to the corner (Figure 11-5). Once 0-2 moves to the corner, pivotman 0-5 moves out to the high post so that he has an opportunity to become part of the play. If 0-5 is clear, 0-1 should pass him the ball. 0-5 can shoot, pass to 0-2 cutting, or pass to 0-4 under.

If in Figure 11-5, point man 0-1 cannot pass the ball to 0-5, he should look to pass the ball to 0-2 in the corner (Figure 11-6). Once point man 0-1 passes the ball to the corner, he triggers our off-side series, which is a continuity offense consisting of 3 options:

Option 1: Hit 0-1 cutting toward the basket (Figure 11-6).
Option 2: Hit 0-5 (Figure 11-7).
Option 3: Pass the ball out to 0-3 (Figure 11-8).

In Figure 11-7, 0-1 passes to 0-2 in the corner, then cuts to the basket. 0-5 takes two steps toward the ball. 0-2 passes to 0-5. 0-5 can shoot, pass to 0-1 under, or pass to 0-4. If 0-2 cannot pass the ball to 0-5, he should dribble out and pass to 0-3.

Figure 11-5

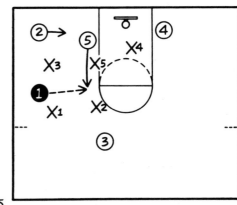

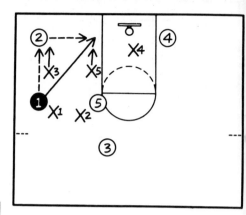

Figure 11-6

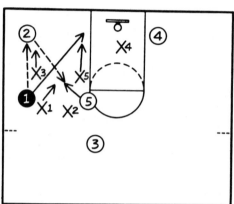

Figure 11-7

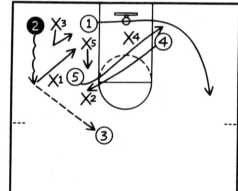

Figure 11-8

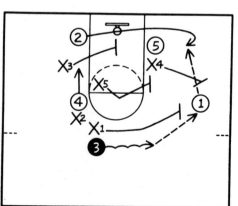

Figure 11-9

In Figure 11-8, after 0-2 dribbles the ball, 0-5 reverses and screens for 0-4. 0-4 breaks to the open space. If 0-2 cannot pass to 0-1 or 0-4, he passes out to 0-3. 0-1 clears to the off side behind 0-5. 0-2 cuts to the basket. 0-3 can shoot, pass to 0-4 or dribble to the off side. Once he dribbles to the off side, he looks to pass the ball to 0-1.

In Figure 11-9, once 0-1 receives the pass he must look for 0-2 setting up next to pivotman 0-5. If 0-1 cannot pass the ball to 0-2, 0-2 moves out to the corner. Once 0-2 moves to the corner, pivotman 0-5 moves out to the high post in the same manner as he did in Figure 11-5. If 0-1 cannot throw the ball to 0-5, he should pass the ball to 0-2 in the corner, triggering our off-side series. Here wing man 0-2 has the same options afforded him, only from the other side of the court, as he had in Figures 11-6, 11-7, and 11-8. The continuity of our off-side series will continue from one side of the court to the other until we get a shot or lose the ball to our opponents.

In our presentation of Play 1 (Figure 11-2), our on-side pivotman 0-4 becomes part of the play by electing to remain stationary in the high post position and waiting for the play to develop. After 0-2 receives a pass from 0-1, pivotman 0-4 can become part of the play by cutting to the basket or by screening away from the ball for 0-5. The factor for determining his action is the defensive position of X-5. If X-5 remains on the inside of 0-4, 0-4 cuts to the basket. If X-5 makes the proper defensive adjustments by positioning himself to the outside of 0-4, 0-4 makes a reverse pivot and screens for 0-5. If 0-4 cuts for the basket but fails to receive the ball, he stays in the low post or clears to the opposite side. If 0-4 clears to the opposite side, 0-5 moves across the foul area to the high post on the strong side (Figure 11-10).

In this situation, if wing man 0-2 cannot pass the ball to pivotman 0-5, he passes the ball out to 0-3, and the offense proceeds in the same manner as outlined in Figures 11-3 through 11-8.

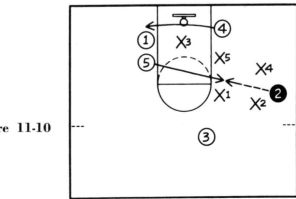

Figure 11-10

PLAY 2: PASS AND CUT, GO TO THE CORNER

Even though we want our point man to put the ball in play on the strong side, Play 2 is listed on our chart as a superior play against a 2-3 zone defense. The objective of this play is to overload one side of the court by sending our point man to the corner. In executing the play, the wing man has five options available:

Option 1: Pass to the point man cutting to the basket (Figure 11-11).
Option 2: Pass to the Pivot (Figure 11-11).
Option 3: Pass to the corner and cut (Figure 11-12).
Option 4: Pass to the corner and move away from the ball (Figure 11-15).

In his first option (Figure 11-11), 0-1 passes to 0-2 and cuts inside 0-4 to the basket. 0-2 passes to 0-1 for a shot. 0-4 rebounds the strong side. 0-5 rebounds the off side. 0-3 moves out to the top of the key. If 0-2 cannot pass the ball to 0-1 under, he looks to pass to 0-4, his second option. If 0-2 cannot pass 0-4 the ball, 0-2 looks to pass to 0-1, his third option, who has cleared to the corner (Figure 11-12). Here 0-2 passes the ball to 0-1 in the corner; 0-2, the first cutter,

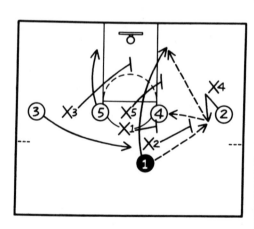

Figure 11-11

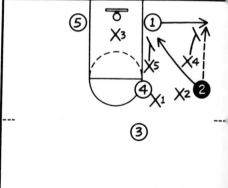

Figure 11-12

cuts to the basket. 0-4, the second cutter, takes two steps toward the ball. 0-5 rebounds the off side. 0-3 protects defensively. 0-1 can pass the ball to the first cutter, 0-2, or the second cutter, 0-4. If point man 0-1 cannot pass the ball to 0-2 cutting, it is because defensive man X-5 has picked him up under. If X-5 is forced to pick up 0-2, then 0-4 should be clear, provided he can stay in front of X-1 who has the defensive responsibility of covering the pivot when the ball is in the corner. If 0-4 can take a position between X-1 and 0-1, 0-1 will pass 0-4 the ball for a shot. Pivotman 0-4 can shoot the ball or pass it to 0-2 or 0-5.

If 0-1 cannot pass the ball to 0-4, he must dribble the ball out of the corner and pass it to 0-3.

In Figure 11-13, once 0-1 dribbles the ball out of the corner, he passes the ball out to 0-3. With such a pass our off-side series is triggered. This is the key for 0-2 to move to the weak side behind 0-4 and for him to break out to receive a pass from 0-3.

In Figure 11-14, 0-3 dribbles the ball over to the off side. 0-2 breaks out to receive a pass from 0-3. 0-1 cuts to the off side and stations himself next to 0-4. 0-3 passes to 0-2, triggering our off-side series. Pivotman 0-5 watches the play develop, then sinks to and rebounds the weak side.

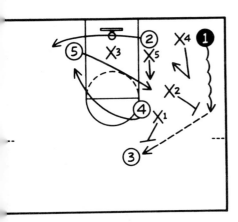

Figure 11-13

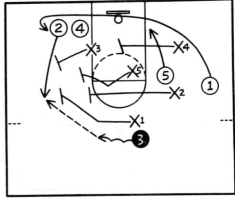

Figure 11-14

Wing man 0-2, after receiving the ball from 0-3, has the following options:

a. He may shoot the ball.
b. He may pass the ball to 0-1 at the side of 0-4 (Figure 11-4).
c. He may pass the ball to 0-5, after 0-5 breaks out to the high post (Figure 11-5).
d. He may pass the ball to 0-1 in the corner (Figure 11-6), who has the same options as illustrated for 0-2 in Figures 11-6, 11-7, and 11-8.

Many good zone defensive teams employ a double-team trap every time the ball is thrown into the corner. If in Play 1 (Figure 11-8), defensive man X-1 were to move down to double up on wing man 0-2, or if in Play 2 (Figure 11-13), defensive man X-2 were to move down to double up on point man 0-1, both offensive players would be at a disadvantage. It is possible that both offensive men could get trapped in the corner to such an extent that they would not be able to dribble the ball out and trigger our off-side series. To combat the double team in the corner, our wing men enter into Option 4: Pass to the corner and move away from the ball.

In Figure 11-15, 0-2 passes to 0-1 in the corner; defensive men X-4 and X-2 double up on 0-1. 0-2 takes two steps out, then watches the play develop. 0-3 cuts to the low post on the strong side. 0-4 takes his customary two steps toward the ball. 0-5 rebounds the weak side.

Whenever X-2 moves down to double up on 0-1, 0-1 has three possible outlet men to whom he can pass the ball: 0-3 under, 0-4 near the pivot, and 0-2. The theory behind the double team is that the two trapping players must never get split. They must never allow the offensive man with the ball to pass the ball between them. The trap in the corner is usually designed to keep 0-1 from passing the ball

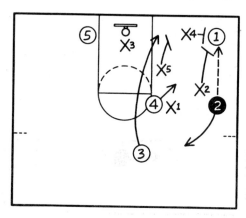

Figure 11-15

to pivotman 0-4. Consequently, if 0-1 doesn't panic he has a good opportunity to get the ball into 0-3 under the basket, or he can easily get the ball out to 0-2. If the pass is made to 0-3, 0-3 should shoot the ball. If the pass is made to 0-2, it triggers our off-side series (Figure 11-16).

After 0-1 passes the ball out to 0-2, 0-2 dribbles the ball over to the the weak side. 0-3 clears to the off side behind 0-5, then breaks up to receive a pass from 0-2. 0-5 watches the play develop. In Figure 11-17, 0-3 receives a pass from 0-2; 0-1 cuts to the off side and stations himself next to 0-5. 0-3 has the same four options available to him as 0-2 had in Figure 11-14.

In Figure 11-15 there is a possibility that wing man 0-2 cannot pass the ball into pivotman 0-4 in the pivot or to point man 0-1 in the corner. Consequently, he may have to pass the ball out to wing man 0-3, triggering our off-side series (Figure 11-18).

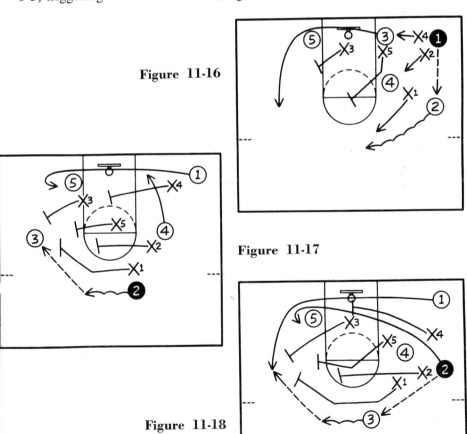

Figure 11-16

Figure 11-17

Figure 11-18

In this play, 0-2 passes the ball out to 0-3. 0-1 clears to the opposite side behind 0-5, then breaks out to receive a pass from 0-3. 0-2 cuts to the off side and stations himself next to 0-5. 0-3 dribbles over and passes the ball to 0-1. 0-4 sinks to and rebounds the weak side. 0-1 has the same four options available to him as 0-3 had in Figure 11-17.

PLAY 3: PASS AND GO BEHIND

The *Go-Behind* is listed in our chart as a superior play against a 2-3 zone defense. It can be run equally well from either the advantage side or the strong side. The play with its six options is successful because it forces a 2-3 zone defensive team to make several quick adjustments in succession. Consequently, whenever the defensive players fail to adjust, an easy shot is made available.

The six options of Play 3, *Pass and Go Behind* are:

Option 1: Hit the pivot cutting toward the basket.
Option 2: Drive toward the basket.
Option 3: Hit the off-side pivotman.
Option 4: Hit the wing man under.
Option 5: Hit the wing man in the corner.
Option 6: Pass the ball out.

Play 3, Pass and Go Behind, Option 1

In Figure 11-19, 0-1 passes to 0-2, cuts to the inside of 0-2 and then as he approaches him at the last instant drops behind him. 0-4 becomes part of the play by cutting toward the basket. 0-2 passes to 0-4. 0-4 shoots and rebounds the strong side. 0-5 sinks to and rebounds the off side. 0-3 protects defensively.

Figure 11-19   **Figure 11-20**

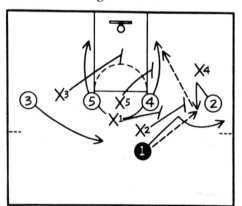
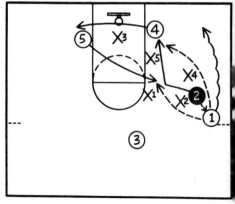

If 0-2 cannot pass the ball to 0-4 cutting, he drops the ball off to 0-1, who has dropped back behind him (Figure 11-20). From this floor position point man 0-1 initiates execution of the remaining five options of the go-behind. Let's examine Option 2, drive toward the basket, and Option 3, hit the off-side pivotman (Figure 11-20).

In Figure 11-20, 0-2 drops the ball off behind him to 0-1, moves to the foul line, pivots on his right foot and cuts to the basket. 0-4 clears to the opposite side. 0-5 breaks to the medium post position on the strong side. 0-1 can drive to the corner looking for a jump shot, drive all the way to the basket for a lay-up or pass the ball to 0-5 in the medium post. If he passes to 0-5, 0-5 shoots. 0-2 rebounds the strong side; 0-4 rebounds the off-side; 0-5 rebounds the shot; 0-3 protects defensively.

If 0-1 drives and X-5 challenges him, he passes off to 0-5. If X-3 challenges his drive he passes off to 0-4.

If 0-1 cannot drive or pass to 0-5 he looks for Option 4, hit the wing man under.

If in Figure 11-20, point man 0-1 cannot pass the ball to 0-2 under the basket or to 0-5 in the medium post, he then looks for 0-2 clearing to the corner and uses Option 5, hit the wing man in the corner (Figure 11-21).

Once 0-2 clears to the corner we have the same alignment as Figure 11-12. Once 0-1 passes to 0-2, 0-2 has the same options that were outlined for 0-1. Here 0-2 looks to pass to the first cutter, 0-1; the second cutter, 0-5; and after dribbling out of the corner, to the third cutter, 0-4. If all three are covered he will use Option 6, pass the ball out, and start our off-side series (Figure 11-14). We will continue working our off-side series until a shot is taken or we lose the ball.

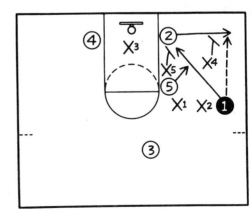

Figure 11-21

PLAY 4: HIT THE PIVOT

Play 4, *Hit the Pivot,* is listed as a superior play on our chart. Previously, in our man-to-man offense, we stated that you must get the ball into the pivot to win. When playing against zone defenses, it is even more important. Here, whenever the ball is thrown into the pivot, all five defensive men are forced to move. It is commonly agreed among coaches that to beat a zone the offensive team must move the defense. We know of no better way to accomplish such movement than to pass the ball into the pivot. The play with the movement that it fosters, along with the four options we have developed from it, has proven to be a very successful play. The four options are as follows:

 Option 1: Hit the wing man cutting backdoor (Figure 11-22).
 Option 2: Hit the point man (Figure 11-22).
 Option 3: Hit the off-side pivotman (Figure 11-22).
 Option 4: Hit the off-side wing man (Figure 11-23).

In Figure 11-22, 0-1 passes to 0-4. 0-2, 0-4's first option, cuts backdoor to the basket. 0-1, 0-4's second option, takes two steps toward the basket, then cuts off 0-4. 0-5 sinks to and rebounds the off side. 0-3 moves out to protect defensively. 0-4 can shoot or pass to 0-2.

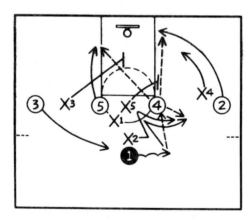

Figure 11-22

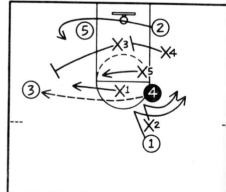

Figure 11-23

If pivotman 0-4 cannot pass the ball to wing man 0-2 cutting back-door, it can only be the result of the defensive play of X-4 or X-5. Pivotman 0-4 would be unable to pass 0-2 the ball if defensive man X-4, playing between 0-2 and the ball, was able to beat 0-2 to the basket. If defensive man X-4 clears to the basket with 0-2 cutting, the floor area he is responsible for defending is left unprotected. Pivot-man 0-4, in possession of the ball and conscious of X-4's position under the basket, passes the ball off to his second option, point man 0-1, for a shot. If pivotman X-5 has to drop off pivotman 0-4 to pick up 0-2 cutting for the basket, 0-4 can shoot, drive or pass the ball to pivotman 0-5 under (Option 3).

If 0-4 cannot pass the ball to point man 0-1, it can only be due to the defensive play of X-2. Defensive man X-2 is the only man who can keep 0-1 from receiving the ball. Therefore, pivotman 0-4 must look to pass the ball to wing man 0-3, his fourth option (Figure 11-23).

In this situation, 0-1 cuts off 0-4; 0-4, unable to pass the ball to 0-2 or 0-1, passes to 0-3, our off-side wing man. 0-2 clears to the offside; 0-5 watches the play develop from his off-side rebounding position. 0-4 sinks to and rebounds the weak side. Wing man 0-3 has the same four options available to him as 0-2 had available to him in Figure 11-14.

The four options available at this point are:

a. Wing man 0-3 can shoot the ball.
b. Wing man 0-3 can pass the ball to wing man 0-2 at the side of 0-5.
c. Wing man 0-3 can pass the ball to 0-5 after 0-5 breaks out to the high post (Figure 11-5).
d. Wing man 0-3 can pass the ball to wing man 0-2 in the corner (Figure 11-6), who has the same options as illustrated in Figures 11-6, 11-7, and 11-8.

PLAY 5: THE GO-PLAY OR THE DRIBBLE OVER

The *Go-Play,* or the Dribble Over, is implemented by point man 0-1 dribbling the ball over to the wing position. It is based on the principle of forcing the defense to pick the offensive men up man-to-man and then enter into an overload alignment. The play consists of the following four options:

Option 1: Hit the off-side pivotman (Figure 11-24).
Option 2: Hit the on-side pivotman (Figure 11-24).
Option 3: Hit the off-side wing man (Figure 11-24).
Option 4: Pass the ball into the corner (Figure 11-25).

In Figure 11-24, 0-1 dribbles the ball over to the right wing position. 0-2 clears the corner. 0-5 breaks to the low post on the strong side. 0-3 sinks to and rebounds the off side. 0-1 passes to 0-5, his first option, for the shot. If 0-1 cannot pass the ball into 0-5, it can only be due to defensive men X-5, X-3, or X-4 picking up 0-5 under.

If X-5 picks up 0-5, 0-1 should pass the ball to the on-side pivotman 0-4, his second option. If X-3 picks up 0-5, 0-1 should pass the ball to the off-side wing man 0-3, his third option. If X-4 picks up 0-5, 0-1 should execute Option 4, a pass into the corner (Figure 11-25).

Once 0-2 gains possession of the ball he can:

a. Shoot the ball.
b. Pass the ball to pivotman 0-5 under (Figure 11-25).
c. Pass the ball to pivotman 0-4 in the pivot (Figure 11-25).
d. Dribble the ball out of the corner and trigger the strong side rotation series (Figure 11-26).

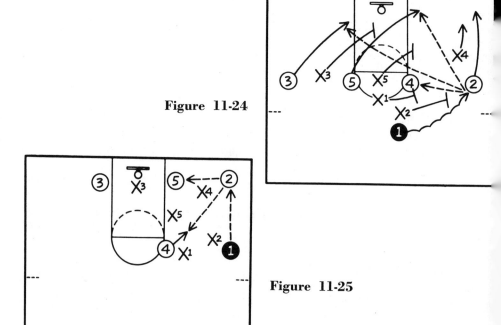

Figure 11-24

Figure 11-25

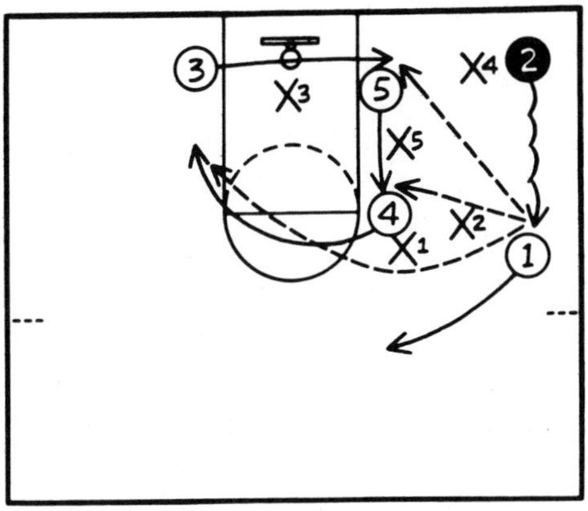

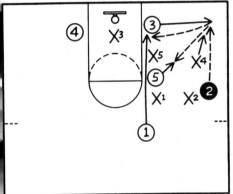

Figure 11-26

Figure 11-27

In Figure 11-26, 0-2 dribbles out of the corner to the foul line extended. 0-1 moves out away from the ball to the right of the circle. 0-4, once 0-2 dribbles, makes a reverse pivot and breaks to the off side replacing 0-3. As 0-2 is dribbling the ball out of the corner, 0-5 moves up from the low post to the high post. 0-3 breaks from the off side to the strong side and if he does not receive a pass from 0-2, he moves to the corner. 0-2 has the following choices:

a. Pass the ball to wing man 0-3 under.
b. Pass the ball to pivotman 0-4 on the weak side.
c. Pass the ball to pivotman 0-5 on the strong side.
d. Pass the ball to 0-3 in the corner and continue with the rotation series.
e. Pass the ball out to point man 0-1 to trigger our weak-side series.

In Figure 11-27, 0-2 decides to pass the ball to 0-3 in the corner. The pass indicated that 0-2 wants to continue the strong side rotation series. 0-1 on the pass to 0-3 breaks to the basket. 0-3 can pass the ball to 0-1 for a shot. If 0-1 shoots, 0-4 rebounds the off side and 0-5 the strong side.

If 0-3 cannot pass the ball to 0-1 under, he can pass the ball to 0-5 in the pivot. If he cannot pass the ball to 0-5, 0-3 will then dribble the ball out to the foul line extended (Figure 11-28).

Now wing man 0-3 has the following four options available:

- *a.* Pass the ball to pivotman 0-4 in the high post on the strong side.
- *b.* Pass the ball to pivotman 0-5 on the weak side.
- *c.* Pass the ball into the corner to 0-1.
- *d.* Pass the ball out to wing man 0-2.

If 0-3 decides to pass the ball out to wing man 0-2, the pass-out will trigger our off-side series (Figure 11-29).

In this series, 0-3 passes to 0-2. 0-1 clears to the off side behind 0-5, then breaks out to receive a pass from 0-2. 0-3 clears to the off side and stations himself next to 0-5. 0-2 dribbles the ball over and passes to 0-1. 0-4 sinks to and rebounds the weak side. 0-1 has the same four options available to him as all the other wing men have had after receiving the second pass in our off-side series, as follows:

- *a.* 0-1 can shoot the ball.
- *b.* 0-1 can pass the ball to 0-3 at the side of pivotman 0-5.

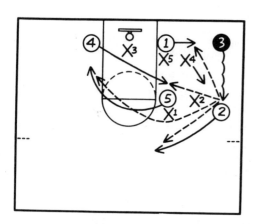

Figure 11-28

Figure 11-29

c. 0-1 can pass the ball to 0-5, after 0-5 breaks out to the high post.

d. 0-1 may pass the ball to 0-3 in the corner.

PLAY 6: THE DRIVE PLAY

Our 1-4 offense includes both a drive from the top of the key and a drive from the wing positions. Let's first consider the drive play from the wing position.

The Wing Drive

The drive from the wing position can be initiated by a wing man anytime he receives a pass from the point man 0-1. Such a drive takes precedence over any play that our point man has previously keyed. Once the wing man drives, the point man must adjust his play to the wing man's drive. The point man must never go to the corner or the side of the drive. If a corner play has been started and the wing drives, the point man must go away from the ball side (Figure 11-30). The

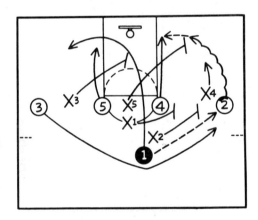

Figure 11-30

drive from the wing is ideally executed from the advantage side. In fact, every time the advantage-side wing man receives a pass, he should immediately drive to the next defensive man and either shoot or pass the ball off to the on-side pivotman (Figure 11-30).

In Figure 11-30, 0-1 passes to 0-2 and cuts to the inside of 0-4. 0-2 drives to the basket looking for the next defensive man, X-5. 0-1, realizing that 0-2 is driving, cuts to the opposite side. As soon as 0-2 starts his drive, 0-4 breaks to the basket. 0-3 moves out to the top of the key, then over toward the wing position to act as a possible outlet

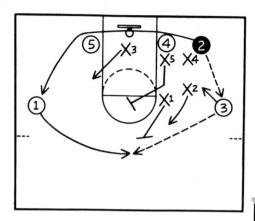

Figure 11-31

Figure 11-32

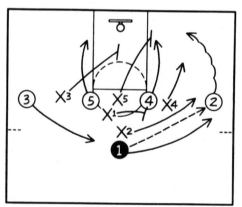

Figure 11-33

Figure 11-34

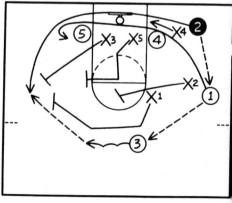

in case 0-2 gets stuck with the ball. 0-5 sinks to and rebounds the off side. If defensive man X-5 adjusts to 0-2's drive and if in the course of his action 0-4 is clear as he cuts to the basket, 0-2 should pass him the ball. If X-5 does not make the adjustment, then 0-2 drives all the way for the shot or a pass to 0-5 on the weak side. Usually in Figure 11-30 defensive man X-4 cannot adjust fast enough to cut off 0-2's drive. However, in the event X-4 is able to keep 0-2 from driving, 0-2 should stop and pass the ball out to 0-3 (Figure 11-31). With such a pass our off-side series is triggered.

In Figure 11-32, wing man 0-2 has the same options available to him as wing man 0-3 had in Figure 11-28.

The drive by the wing man is best accomplished whenever point man 0-1 realizes that the wing man on the advantage side has a drive opportunity. Under such circumstances, point man 0-1 can pass the ball to the wing man and move to the wing position to act as an outlet.

In Figure 11-33, if 0-2 cannot shoot or pass the ball inside, he can pass the ball to 0-1, triggering our off-side series.

In Figure 11-34, 0-2 triggers the off-side series as he passes out to 0-1. 0-2 clears to the off side behind 0-5, then breaks up to receive a pass from 0-3. 0-1 passes out to 0-3 and cuts to the off side, stationing himself next to 0-5. 0-3 passes to 0-2. 0-4 rebounds the weak side. 0-5 rebounds the strong side. Wing man 0-2 has the same options available to him as 0-1 had in Figure 11-29.

The Drive Play from the Point Position

This play is listed on our chart as a superior play against a 2-3 zone defense. Earlier in our man-to-man offense, the *Drive Play* was our big play. It was the one play we went to whenever we were in need of a basket. Here in our zone offense, even though it is listed as a superior play, it is not our best play. What it does for our zone offense is keep the defense honest. Any time a zone defense matches up and plays us man-to-man, we counteract with the use of our drive play and its four options:

Option 1: Hit the off-side pivotman (Figure 11-35).
Option 2: Shoot or drive.
Option 3: Hit the on-side pivotman rolling to the basket (Figure 11-35).
Option 4: Hit the wing man (Figure 11-35).

In Figure 11-35, 0-4 moves out, sets a screen on X-2, then rolls to

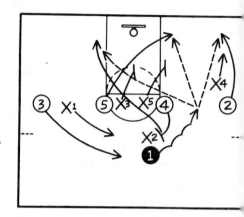

Figure 11-35

the off side. 0-5 breaks from the high post to the low post on the strong side. 0-2 sinks to the baseline. 0-3 takes two steps out and protects defensively. 0-1 looks to pass to his first option, pivotman 0-5; his third option, pivotman 0-4, or his fourth option, wing man 0-2 in the corner.

If point man 0-1 cannot pass the ball to 0-5, it can only be the result of defensive man X-3's moving over and cutting him off or because X-5 has dropped back and picked up 0-5. If defensive man X-5 drops back to pick up 0-5, point man 0-1 enters into Option 2, in which he can either shoot or drive to the basket. If X-3 picks up pivotman 0-5, point man 0-1 enters into Option 3 and passes to 0-4 rolling to the off side.

If point man 0-1 drives off the screen, defensive man X-4 could possibly move over to cut 0-1 off. This happens quite frequently, especially when 0-1 drives. If defensive man X-4 jumps out and picks up 0-1, point man 0-1 must enter into Option 4, and pass to 0-2 in the corner. 0-2 can shoot, drive, or pass to 0-5 under.

This concludes our discussion of the basic six against the 2-3 zone defense. We are now ready to consider the basic six against the 1-3-1 zone defense.

12

THE BASIC SIX

AGAINST THE 1-3-1 ZONE DEFENSE

The basic six have been challenged by the 1-3-1 zone defense more than by any other type zone over the last two years. This is primarily due to the success of the various colleges and universities over the country who have been employing the 1-3-1. Its popularity has filtered down from the college level to the high school level and accounts for our seeing so much of it lately.

The basic difference between the 1-3-1 zone defense and the 2-3 zone defense, in regard to our 1-4 offense, is that the base line man in the 1-3-1 takes away our play from the corners. Our strategy in attacking the defense, even though it is somewhat unorthodox, is to design our plays to cope with the defensive play of the baseline man. Our attack differs from others in that most teams try to attack the 1-3-1 zone by designing their plays to cope with the defensive play of the point man. The offensive tactics we employ in attacking the baseline man include various means by which we attempt to isolate him on the strong side and set a screen on him as the ball moves over to the weak side. These tactics will be explained fully as the chapter unfolds. The offensive chart for the basic six when challenged by a 1-3-1 zone defense is as follows:

TYPE ZONE DEFENSE: 1-3-1   TYPE OFFENSE: 1-4

Bad Plays	Mediocre Plays	Superior Plays
Play 6: The Drive by the Wing Man.	Play 1: Pass and Cut, Clear to the Opposite Side. Play 2: Pass and Cut, Go to the Corner.	Play 3: Go Behind. Play 4: Hit the Pivot. Play 5: Dribble Over. Play 6: The Drive by the Point Man.

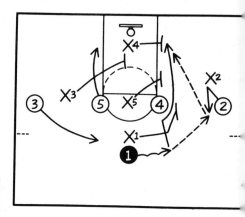

Figure 12-1

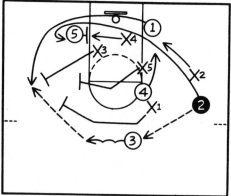

Figure 12-2

PLAY 1: PASS AND CUT, CLEAR TO
THE OPPOSITE SIDE

The *Pass and Cut, Clear to the Opposite Side* is listed on our chart as a mediocre play, primarily because the play is of little practical value on the strong side. It is strictly a weak-side play. It is of little value on the strong side because it is hard for us to isolate the baseline man where we would like to contain him on the side of the court where the ball is first put into play. What the play really does on the strong side is to isolate the baseline man in a floor position close to the basket. This is the worst possible place for us to contain him. For us to have a successful play it is essential that we force the baseline man away from the basket. Our pass and cut doesn't accomplish this, and, consequently, the play on this side of the court is of little value.

In Figure 12-1, since 0-1 has little opportunity to shoot the ball after receiving a pass from 0-2, chances are good that 0-2 would never pass him the ball. With 0-2's first option taken away from him by the play of defensive man X-4, 0-2 has two options left; a pass to 0-4 or a pass to 0-3 which will trigger our off-side series.

In Figure 12-2, 0-1, after failing to receive a return pass from 0-2, clears to the opposite side. 0-2 passes the ball out to 0-3, triggering our off-side offense. 0-3 passes to 0-1. 0-2 cuts behind 0-5. 0-5 screens defensive man X-4. 0-4 sinks to and rebounds the weak side. 0-1 can shoot, or pass the ball to 0-2, 0-5 or 0-3.

Pivotman 0-5's screen of baseline man X-4 illustrates our strategy of attacking the 1-3-1 zone defense by screening the baseline man as the ball moves over to the weak side. If the screen is successful, 0-2 should have an easy close-to-the-basket jump shot. If defensive man X-4 overcomes the screen set on him, 0-5 could momentarily be clear. If he is, point man 0-1 should pass the ball to him. If 0-5 is not clear, it can only be due to the defensive play of X-5. Defensive man X-5 would have to pick up 0-5, since defensive man X-4 is already engaged in defending 0-2. Once 0-5 realizes he is not going to receive a pass, he moves out to the top of the key (Figure 12-3). When he does, 0-1 can pass him the ball. When in Figure 12-2, 0-2 does not receive the ball from 0-1, 0-2 clears to the corner (Figure 12-3).

Once 0-2 gets to the corner, 0-1 can pass him the ball. As he passes him the ball, defensive man X-4 is forced to the corner also. With X-4 isolated in the corner, 0-2 has the following options:

Option 1: Hit 0-1 cutting to the basket (Figure 12-3).
Option 2: Hit 0-5 (Figure 12-3).
Option 3: Pass the ball out to 0-3 (Figure 12-4).

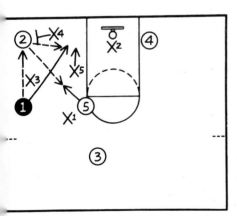

Figure 12-3

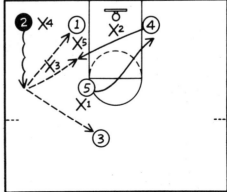

Figure 12-4

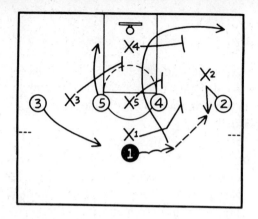

Figure 12-5

If in Figure 12-3, 0-2 cannot pass the ball to 0-1 or 0-5, 0-2 will dribble the ball out (Figure 12-4). As he dribbles the ball out, defensive men X-4, X-3, and X-5 are forced into making certain decisions. X-4 must decide how far out he is going to stay with 0-2. X-3 must decide just when he is going to pick up 0-2. X-5 must decide when he is going to leave 0-1 standing under the basket and when he must pick up 0-4. If X-4 leaves 0-2 too soon, 0-2 could possibly shoot the ball. If X-2 picks up 0-3 too soon, 0-5 may be clear. If X-5 picks up 0-5 too soon, 0-1 could be clear for a shot. If 0-1 and 0-5 are both covered, 0-2 passes the ball out to 0-3, and the off-side series proceeds on the opposite side.

PLAY 2: PASS AND CUT, GO TO THE CORNER

Play 2, *Pass and Cut, Go to the Corner,* is listed on our chart as a superior play, because whenever point man 0-1 cuts to the corner, defensive man X-4 must move to the corner with him, and when X-4 moves to the corner, he has been isolated. Consequently, the corner play isolates the baseline man on the strong side of the court (Figure 12-6).

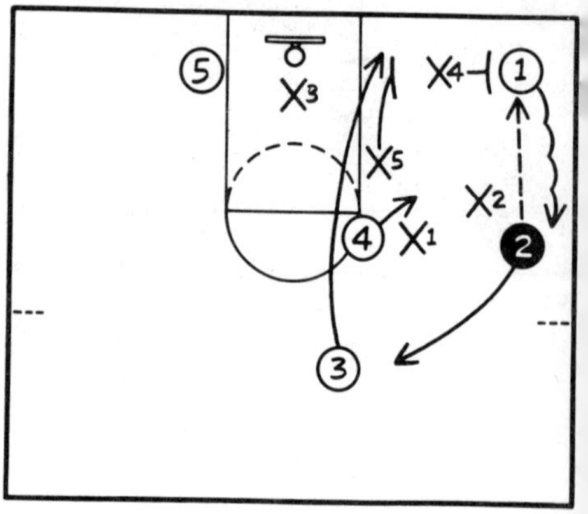

Figure 12-6

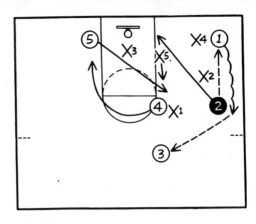

Figure 12-7

Once the ball is passed to 0-2, 0-2 can pass the ball to 0-1, 0-4, or out to 0-3. If he passes the ball to 0-4, 0-4 can shoot or pass the ball to 0-5. If 0-2 passes the ball to 0-1 in the corner, 0-1 has the same options available to him as 0-2 did in Figures 12-3 and 12-4. In addition to these options, 0-1 must be aware of 0-2 passing him the ball, and instead of cutting toward the basket, must retain his floor position or move out away from the ball toward the top of the key (Figure 12-6). Such a maneuver by 0-2 usually occurs whenever point man 0-1 is being double-teamed by defensive men X-4 and X-2 (Figure 12-6).

If in Figure 12-6, point man 0-1 dribbles the ball out of the corner, the dribble will key our strong side rotation series, which involve changes in floor positions between 0-1, 0-3, and 0-2 as well as between 0-4 and 0-5. The strong side rotation series has been previously outlined in Figures 11-27 and 11-28; consequently it will not be necessary for us to outline it again in this chapter.

If in Figure 12-6, 0-1 does not pass the ball to 0-3 under, 0-3, after 0-1 dribbles, moves to the corner. 0-1 can pass the ball to him and continue our rotation series by moving away from the ball, or he can cut to the basket as he did in Figure 12-3. If 0-1 cannot pass the ball to 0-3 in the corner, he can trigger our off-side series by passing the ball out to 0-2. The corner play sets up the screen on the weak side on X-4, the baseline man. In Figure 12-5, X-4 goes to the corner with 0-1. If 0-2 passes to 0-1 in the corner and cuts to the basket, 0-1 has the same options available to him as 0-2 had in Figures 12-3 and 12-4. For 0-1 to trigger our off-side series he must dribble out of the corner and pass the ball out to 0-3 (Figure 12-7).

In this play, 0-2 passes to 0-1, then cuts to the basket. 0-4 takes one step toward the ball. 0-1 dribbles the ball out. 0-4 reverse pivots and clears to the opposite side. 0-5 breaks toward the ball. 0-1 passes to 0-3.

The off-side series continues in Figure 12-8 with 0-3 dribbling the ball over to the off side. 0-2 clears to the opposite side, then breaks up to receive a pass from 0-3. 0-1 cuts to the basket, then clears to the off side behind 0-4. 0-4 sets a screen on defensive man X-4. 0-3 passes to 0-2. 0-2 has the same options available to him as 0-1 had in Figure 12-3.

PLAY 3: THE GO-BEHIND

Play 3, the *Go-Behind* is listed on our chart as a superior play. It contains the following attributes necessary for its superior classification:

1. The capability of isolating the baseline man on the strong side.
2. The capability of screening the baseline man as the ball swings over from the strong side to the weak side.

Although the play has the following six options, we will only outline those that are actually responsible for the isolation of the baseline man and those options that include a screen on the baseline man.

Option 1: Hit the pivotman cutting toward the basket.
Option 2: A drive toward the basket.
Option 3: Hit the off-side pivotman.
Option 4: Hit the wing man under.
Option 5: Hit the wing man in the corner.
Option 6: Pass the ball out.

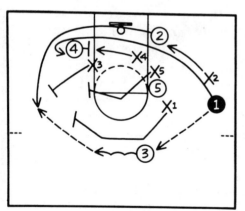

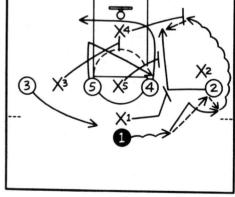

Figure 12-8   **Figure 12-9**

Let us first investigate the manner in which the *Go-Behind* implements the isolation of the baseline man, and then consider how the various options implement the screen on him. The options we will consider are 2, 5, and 6 listed above.

In Figure 12-9, 0-1 passes to 0-2 and cuts to the inside of him; then as he approaches 0-2, at the last instant drops behind him. 0-4 cuts toward the basket and clears to the opposite side. 0-2 drops the ball off behind him to 0-1; then he moves to the foul line, pivots on his right foot, and cuts to the basket. 0-5 sinks toward the basket, then cuts toward the ball on the strong side. 0-1 receives the ball and drives toward X-4. 0-1 shoots the ball or passes off to 0-2 if X-4 challenges him. 0-4 rebounds the weak side. 0-3 breaks out to the top of the key. 0-5 rebounds the strong side.

Point man 0-1's drive toward defensive man X-4 isolates X-4, making it possible for 0-2 to get in behind him for a possible shot. If 0-1 decides not to drive and does not pass the ball to (*a*) his first option, 0-4, cutting to the basket; or (*b*) his third option, 0-5, the off-side pivotman; or (*c*) his fourth option 0-2 under, he can then look to pass the ball to his fifth option, 0-2, in the corner (Figure 12-10).

In Figure 12-10, 0-2 drops the ball off behind him to 0-1; then he moves to the foul line, pivots on his right foot, cuts to the basket, and clears to the corner. 0-1 passes to 0-2. 0-5 maintains his position and watches the play develop. 0-4 rebounds the off side. 0-3 remains at the top of the key and protects defensively.

In Figure 12-11, 0-1's pass to 0-2 isolates defensive man X-4 in the

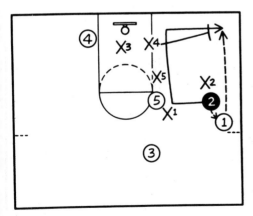

Figure 12-10

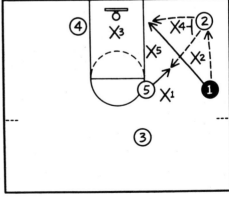

Figure 12-11

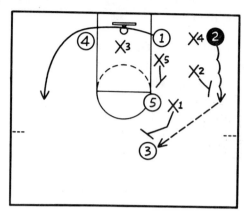

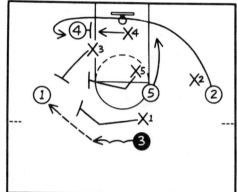

Figure 12-12

Figure 12-13

corner. After 0-1 passes to 0-2, 0-1 cuts to the basket. Wing man 0-2 can pass the ball to 0-1 under or to 0-5 in the pivot, or he can dribble the ball out and pass the ball to 0-3. If 0-2 passes to 0-1 under, 0-1 can shoot or pass to 0-5. If 0-2 passes to 0-5, 0-5 can shoot, pass the ball to 0-1, or pass the ball to 0-4. If 0-2 passes the ball out to 0-3, he triggers the off-side series (Figure 12-12). The pass-out also acts as the key for pivotman 0-4 to set a screen on the baseline man, X-4 (Figure 12-13).

In Figure 12-13, 0-3 dribbles toward the weak side and passes to 0-1. 0-2 clears to the weak side behind 0-4. 0-4 sets a screen on defensive man X-4. 0-5 sinks to and rebounds the weak side. 0-1, with the same options as he had in Figure 12-3, can:

    a. Pass to 0-2 cutting behind 0-4.
    b. Pass to 0-2 clearing to the corner.
    c. Pass to 0-4 under.
    d. Pass to 0-4 as he breaks out to the high post.
    e. Pass the ball out to 0-3, triggering the weak-side series.

In Figure 12-10, 0-1 can start the off-side series, **Option 6**, immediately by passing the ball out to wing man 0-3 instead of passing to 0-2 in the corner. When he does (Figure 12-14), 0-2 clears to the opposite side, cuts behind 0-4, then breaks up to receive a pass from 0-3. 0-1 cuts to the basket, then clears to the opposite side behind 0-4. 0-4 sets a screen on X-4. 0-3 passes to 0-2. 0-5 sinks to and rebounds the weak side. 0-2 has the same options available to him as 0-1 had in Figure 12-2.

PLAY 4: HIT THE PIVOT

Play 4, *Hit the Pivot* is listed as a superior play on our chart. The four options of play 4 are very effective against the 1-3-1 zone defense. We will consider them in regard to how they isolate the baseline man on the strong side, and how they bring about a screen on him from the weak side. The four options of this play are:

Option 1: Hit the wing man cutting backdoor.
Option 2: Hit the off-side pivotman.
Option 3: Hit the point man.
Option 4: Hit the off-side wing man.

In Figure 12-15, the pass into pivotman 0-4 puts tremendous pressure on defensive man X-4. With 0-2 and 0-5 both breaking to the basket at the same time, defensive man X-4 isolates himself toward one or the other. Pivotman 0-4 must be aware of the situation and pass the ball to the man cutting who is not being challenged by X-4. If 0-4 passes the ball to 0-5, Option 2 has been initiated and 0-5 shoots the ball. If 0-4 cannot pass the ball to 0-2 or 0-5, he looks for Option 3, a pass to point man 0-1. If 0-4 cannot make a pass to 0-2, 0-5, or 0-1, he enters into Option 4, hit the off-side wing man (Figure 12-16). Option 4 will illustrate the manner in which the screen on the baseline man is put into effect.

Figure 12-14

Figure 12-15

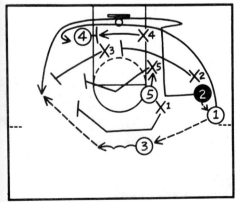

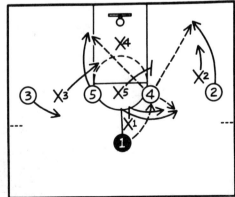

In Figure 12-16, 0-4 passes to 0-3. 0-2 clears to the opposite side cutting behind 0-5. 0-5 sets a screen on baseline man X-4. 0-1 moves out to the top of the key to protect defensively. 0-4, after passing to 0-3, sinks to and rebounds the weak side. 0-3 can shoot the ball, pass to 0-2 at the side of 0-5, pass to 0-5, or pass to 0-2 in the corner. If 0-3 passes the ball to 0-2 in the corner, 0-2 has the same options available to him as he did in Figures 12-3 and 12-4.

PLAY 5: THE DRIBBLE OVER

The *Dribble Over* is one of the most successful plays we have available in our 1-4 offense to use against a 1-3-1 zone defense. Its four options give us several opportunities to isolate the baseline man on the strong side. They also afford us methods for triggering our off-side series from which we can get a screen on the baseline man as the ball moves from the strong side of the court to the weak side. The four options, as illustrated in Figure 12-17, are:

Option 1: Hit the off-side pivotman.
Option 2: Hit the on-side pivotman.
Option 3: Hit the off-side wing man.
Option 4: Pass the ball into the corner.

In Figure 12-17, whenever wing man 0-2 clears to the corner, defensive man X-4 must challenge him. Such defensive coverage isolates

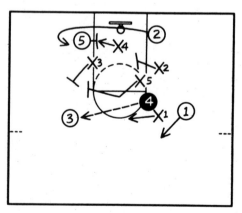

Figure 12-16

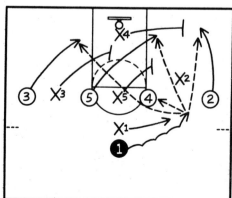

Figure 12-17

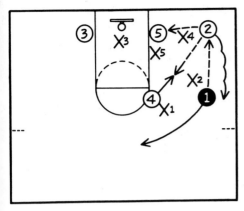

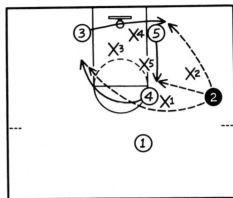

Figure 12-18

Figure 12-19

X-4 momentarily, enabling 0-1 to make a quick pass to 0-5. If 0-1 cannot pass to 0-5 it is only because Option 1 can be defended against successfully in the following ways:

1. Defensive man X-5 drops back to pick up 0-5 as he cuts to the basket.
2. Defensive man X-3 picks up 0-5 as he cuts to the basket.
3. Defensive man X-4 maintains his position under the basket and picks up 0-5 as he cuts.

If defensive man X-5 drops back to pick up 0-5 as he cuts to the basket, point man 0-1 should enter into Option 2, hit the on-side pivotman (Figure 12-17).

If point man 0-1 passes the ball to pivotman 0-4, pivotman 0-4 can shoot the ball, pass it to 0-5 under on the strong side, or pass the ball to wing man 0-3 under on the weak side. If in Figure 12-17, defensive man X-3 picks up 0-5 as he cuts for the basket, point man 0-1 should enter into Option 3, hit the off-side wing man.

If defensive man X-4 maintains his position under the basket, and picks up 0-5 as he cuts, point man 0-1 should enter into Option 4, pass the ball into the corner (Figure 12-18).

In Figure 12-18, point man 0-1 passes the ball to wing man 0-2 into the corner. Wing man 0-2 should shoot the ball. If he cannot shoot the ball, he can pass to 0-5 under, pass to 0-4 in the pivot, or dribble the ball out. If wing man 0-2 decides to dribble the ball out, he can trigger our strong side rotation series (Figure 12-19) or our off-side series (Figure 12-21).

183

In Figure 12-19, wing man 0-2 after dribbling out of the corner, can:

a. Pass the ball to wing man 0-3 under.

b. Pass the ball to pivotman 0-4 on the weak side.

c. Pass the ball to pivotman 0-5 in the high post on the strong side.

d. Pass the ball to 0-3 in the corner and continue working the rotation series (Figure 12-20).

e. Pass the ball out to point man 0-1 to trigger our off-side series.

In Figure 12-20, wing man 0-3 can pass the ball to point man 0-1, he can pass the ball to 0-5, or he can dribble the ball out of the corner to the foul line extended and continue working the strong side rotation series.

If 0-2 cannot pass the ball to 0-3 in the corner, he can pass the ball out and trigger our off-side series (Figure 12-21), the method by which we screen the baseline man as he the ball moves from the strong side over to the weak side.

In Figure 12-21, 0-2 passes out to 0-1. 0-3 clears to the off-side behind 0-5, then breaks out to receive a pass from 0-1. 0-2 cuts to the basket and clears to the opposite side, stationing himself next to 0-4. 0-1 passes to 0-3. 0-4 sets a screen on defensive man X-4. 0-5 sinks to and rebounds the weak side. 0-3 has the same four options available to him as he had in Figure 12-16.

PLAY 6: THE DRIVE PLAY

On our chart we have placed the *Drive by the Wing Man* as part of Play 6. Actually, this play can be used at any time and as a part of

Figure 12-20   **Figure 12-21**

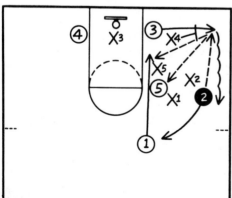

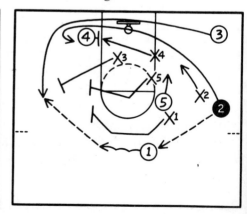

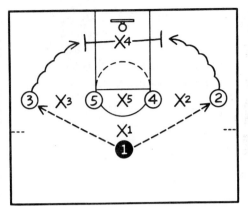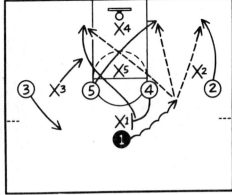

Figure 12-22   **Figure 12-23**

any one of our plays. We placed it here as part of Play 6 so that we can discuss its merits when used for attacking the 1-3-1 zone defense. On our chart the drive by the wing man is classified as a bad play because the baseline man in the 1-3-1 zone will always be in position to shut off any drive attempt (Figure 12-22).

In this situation, baseline man X-4's defensive position gains the defensive advantage. Offensively the odds for securing a percentage shot are not favorable. Consequently, when facing a 1-3-1 zone, the drive by a wing man in our 1-4 offense is discouraged.

On the other hand, Play 6, the *Drive By The Point Man,* is listed on our chart as a superior play, and its use in attacking a 1-3-1 zone defense is often encouraged. The four options it affords us make it possible for us to gain several good percentage shots. They help to isolate the baseline man on the strong side as well as enable us to set a screen on him as the ball moves over from the strong side to the weak side of the court. The four options we will discuss are:

Option 1: Hit the off-side pivotman.
Option 2: Shoot or drive.
Option 3: Hit the on-side pivotman rolling to the basket.
Option 4: Hit the wing man.

Figure 12-23, illustrates the four options of Play 6, the *Drive Play.* Here 0-4 moves out to screen defensive man X-1, pivots on his right foot, and rolls to the off side. 0-1 drives off the screen. 0-5 cuts to the basket. 0-2 clears to the corner. 0-3 moves out to the top of the key and protects defensively. 0-1 can shoot, drive to the basket, or pass to 0-5, 0-4 or 0-2, depending upon the play of baseline man X-4. If X-4 decides to pick up 0-2 clearing to the corner, 0-1 will enter

185

into Option 1 by passing the ball to pivotman 0-5. If defensive man X-4 picks up 0-5 cutting to the basket, point man 0-1 can enter into Option 3 by passing the ball to pivotman 0-4 rolling to the basket. If baseline man X-4 picks up 0-5 and defensive man X-2 picks up 0-1 driving, 0-1 should enter into Option 4 by passing the ball to wing man 0-2 clearing to the corner. In each case the offensive player receiving the ball should have a shooting opportunity. The only exception could be in Option 4. If wing man 0-2 cannot shoot the ball, he could pass the ball to pivotman 0-5 under or pass the ball out to wing man 0-3, triggering our off-side series.

This concludes our discussion of the basic six against the 1-3-1 zone defense. Each of the plays listed as a superior one on our offensive rating chart has met the criteria set up earlier. They adhere to the offensive tactics of attacking the baseline man by isolating him on the strong side and setting a screen on him as the ball moves from the strong side of the court to the weak side. We are now ready to discuss the basic six against the 1-2-2 zone defense.

13

THE BASIC SIX

AGAINST THE 1-2-2 ZONE DEFENSE

We attack the 1-2-2 zone defense with tactics similar to those of the basic six against the 1-3-1 zone defense. Here in the 1-2-2 zone defense, we attempt to isolate the defensive man on the strong side and set a screen on him as the ball moves away and over to the weak side of the court. The primary differences between the two defenses as viewed in relation to our 1-4 offense are:

1. The 1-2-2 zone defense has two baseline men, whereas the 1-3-1 zone has one.
2. The 1-2-2 zone defense assigns pivot responsibilities to both of its wing men, whereas the wing men in the 1-3-1 zone have none.

To cope with these differences, we are forced to broaden the isolation and screening concepts that we presented earlier in Chapter 11. We have extended our isolation views to include the wing man on the strong side as well as the baseline man. We have expanded our screening sentiments to include the screening of either one of our baseline men, depending upon which one is defending the weak side.

The discussions that follow will explain in detail how these broadened concepts, along with the basic six, help to successfully attack the 1-2-2 zone defense.

The offensive chart for our basic six when employed against the 1-2-2 zone defense is as follows:

TYPE DEFENSE: 1-2-2   TYPE OFFENSE: 1-4

Bad Plays	Mediocre Plays	Superior Plays
None.	Play 1: Pass-and-Cut, Clear to the Opposite Side.	Play 2: Pass-and-Cut, Go to the Corner. Play 3: Go-Behind. Play 4: Hit the Pivot. Play 5: Dribble Over. Play 6: The Drive Play.

PLAY 1: PASS-AND-CUT, CLEAR TO THE OPPOSITE SIDE

The *Pass-and-Cut, Clear to the Opposite Side* is again listed on our offensive rating chart as a mediocre play. The play is, however, con-

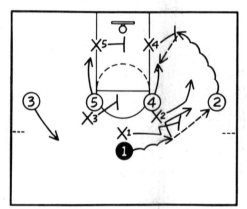

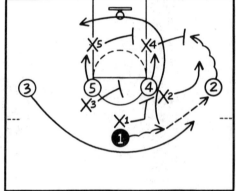

Figure 13-1   Figure 13-2

siderably more effective against the 1-2-2 zone defense than it is against the 1-3-1 zone. This is due primarily to the fact that the defensive wing men in the 1-2-2 must defense the pivot area as well as the wings. Consequently, our offensive wing men have many more drive opportunities available to them here than they had available in the 1-3-1.

These added drive opportunities are not only made available to our wing men as they execute Play 1, but they also present themselves every time a wing man receives a pass from a man in the point position.

In Figure 13-1, 0-1 passes to 0-2, then cuts toward the basket. 0-2 drives the baseline to the next defensive man, X-4. 0-4 breaks to the basket. 0-1, realizing 0-2 is driving, veers off toward the wing position.

0-5 sinks to and rebounds the weak side. 0-3 moves to the top of the key. 0-2 shoots or passes to 0-4.

If point man 0-1 is slow in realizing that 0-2 is driving, 0-1 may not be able to veer his cut to the basket. In such cases he can stop in the pivot area or clear to the opposite side. If he clears to the opposite side, wing man 0-3 must come over from his point position to help out 0-2 if 0-2 gets stuck with the ball (Figure 13-2).

If wing man 0-2 cannot shoot or pass the ball to 0-4, he turns and looks to the outlet position for wing man 0-3 (Figure 13-3). Once wing man 0-2 passes the ball out to 0-3, 0-3 can trigger the off-side series by passing the ball out to point man 0-1.

Now 0-2 clears to the opposite side. 0-1 moves to the top of the key. 0-3 passes out to 0-1 and cuts to the basket. 0-5 rebounds the weak side. 0-4 watches the play develop. In Figure 13-4, 0-3 clears to

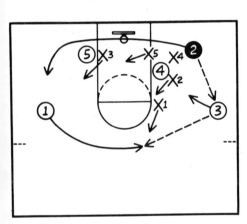

Figure 13-3

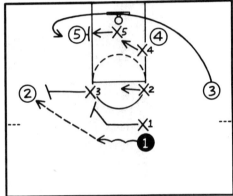

Figure 13-4

the off side behind 0-5. 0-1 passes to 0-2. 0-5 sets a screen on defensive man X-5. 0-4 rebounds the weak side. 0-2 can shoot or pass to 0-3, 0-5, or 0-1.

In analyzing the 1-2-2 zone defense, the pivot area seems to be the most vulnerable point of attack. We believe that the defense does not protect the pivot area as well as it should be defended. Consequently, it is often to our advantage for 0-2, in Figure 13-2, to pass up the drive opportunity in the hope of passing the ball to 0-4 in the pivot or to 0-3 who can in turn pass it into 0-4. If wing man 0-3 cannot pass the ball into 0-4, he will bring the ball over and enter into the off-side series.

PLAY 2: PASS-AND-CUT, GO TO THE CORNER

Play 2, *Pass-and-Cut, Go to the Corner,* is listed in our offensive rating chart as a superior play because it isolates both the baseline man and the wing man on the strong side and provides us with an opportunity to screen the baseline man as the ball swings over from the strong side to the weak side of the court.

Once the ball is passed to the wing man, he has the following five options:

Option 1: Pass to the point man cutting (Figure 13-5).
Option 2: Pass to the on-side pivotman (Figure 13-5).
Option 3: Pass to the corner and cut toward the basket.
Option 4: Pass to the corner and initiate the rotation series.
Option 5: Pass the ball out.

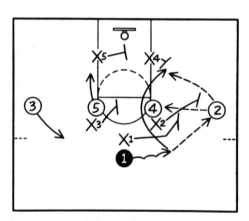

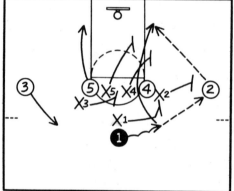

Figure 13-5   **Figure 13-6**

In Figure 13-5, point man 0-1 is very seldom clear enough to receive a pass as he is cutting for the basket. Defensive man X-4 is usually in such a position that he discourages a pass into 0-1 cutting, and in the event 0-1 receives a pass, X-4 can easily keep him from shooting.

In spite of such circumstances, we continue to include Option 1 in our offense for two primary purposes. First, there is always the possibility that 0-1 can catch defensive man X-4 out of position, and an easy shot may develop. Second, in the event we must face a match-up zone defense, Option 1 can be a great asset to our offense (Figure 13-6).

If 0-2 cannot shoot the ball or pass to 0-4, he passes to 0-1 in the corner (Figure 13-7). Here point man 0-1 can pass the ball to 0-2 cutting for the basket, or to pivotman 0-4. Pivotman 0-4 has a very good chance of being clear, especially if X-2 is slow in cutting off the passing lane. Pivotman 0-4's chances of being clear are greatly increased by the play of wing man 0-2. Whenever wing man 0-2 cuts for the basket, if he does not receive a return pass he stops at the side of X-5. This movement, or lack of it, isolates defensive man X-5 to such an extent that he cannot prevent 0-4 from shooting the ball.

If in Figure 13-7, point man 0-1 cannot pass the ball to 0-2 or 0-4, 0-1 dribbles the ball out to the foul line extended and passes the ball to wing man 0-3. With such a pass 0-1 triggers our off-side series (Figure 13-8), and 0-2 clears to the weak side behind 0-5, then breaks out to receive a pass from 0-3. In this maneuver, 0-2 clears to the off side behind 0-5. 0-3 passes to 0-2. 0-5 sets a screen on defensive man X-5. 0-4 rebounds the weak side. 0-2 can pass the ball to 0-2, 0-5, or 0-3.

If in Figure 13-8, wing man 0-2 passes the ball out to 0-3, the pass

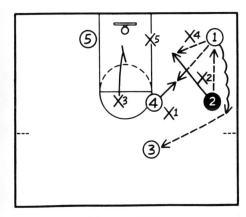

Figure 13-7

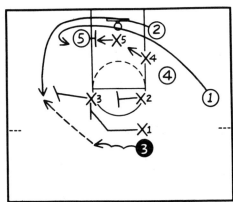

Figure 13-8

triggers our weak-side series. We will continue with this continuity until a shot is secured.

In Figure 13-7 there is a possibility that wing man 0-2, after passing the ball to point man 0-1 in the corner, may decide to initiate the strong-side rotation series. If he does, the play will proceed in the same manner as described in Chapter 11 (Figures 11-27 and 11-28).

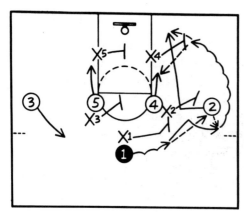

Figure 13-9

Figure 13-10

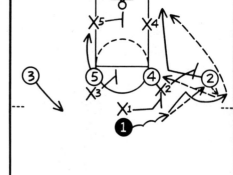

PLAY 3: THE GO-BEHIND

Play 3, the *Go-Behind,* is listed on our offensive rating chart as a superior play. It adheres to the criteria we set up earlier for such plays in our 1-4 offense for attacking a 1-2-2 zone defense.

The five options we will discuss of Play 3, the *Go-Behind* are:

Option 1: The drive by the point man.
Option 2: Hit the wing man under.
Option 3: Hit the pivotman.
Option 4: Hit the wing man in the corner.
Option 5: Pass the ball out.

Figure 13-9 illustrates Option 1, the drive by the point man. Here 0-1 passes to 0-2. 0-1 cuts to the inside of 0-2, and as he approaches 0-2 drops behind him at the last instant. 0-2 drops the ball off behind him to 0-1, moves to the foul line, pivots on his right foot, and cuts to the basket. 0-5 sinks to and rebounds the weak side. 0-3 moves out to the top of the key. 0-1 drives the baseline and can shoot a jump shot or pass off to 0-2 or 0-4.

Figure 13-10 illustrates Option 2, hit the wing man under. Here

192

after 0-2 drops the ball off behind him to point man 0-1, he moves to the foul line, pivots on his right foot, and cuts for the basket. The influencing factor in 0-2's receiving a return from 0-1 is the play of defensive man X-4. If X-4 moves away from his position under the basket, either toward the corner or toward 0-4, 0-1 can successfully pass 0-2 the ball. If defensive man X-4 retains his position near the basket, 0-1 has little chance of passing 0-2 the ball. In such cases, 0-1 should look first to pivotman 0-4 because he may clear for a shot, or if he is defended, he is being defended by X-1. Naturally if 0-4 is clear, 0-1 will pass the ball to him for a shot (Option 3). If 0-4 is defended, it is by point man X-1; this is advantageous because X-1 would be much smaller than 0-4. Furthermore, defensive man X-1 must not only try to defend 0-4, but in the event 0-2 passes 0-3 the ball X-1 must also defend 0-3. This really gives defensive man X-1 more than he can adequately handle, and therefore he is prone to make mistakes. If, for example, 0-1 fakes a pass out to 0-3, X-1 will usually take a step or two toward 0-3. When this occurs, 0-4 is clear; 0-2 can then pass him the ball for a short jump shot.

If 0-4 is going to be defended adequately once the ball is passed to 0-1, he must be defended by X-4. If X-4 picks up 0-4, then 0-2 will be clear under the basket unless defensive man X-5 picks him up. If X-5 picks up 0-2 under, then 0-2 should move to the corner (Figure 13-11). Defensive man X-5 will not follow 0-2 to the corner because his defensive responsibilities never call for such action. Defending the corner is X-4's responsibility. Consequently, it is a relatively easy task for 0-1 to pass the ball to 0-2 in the corner.

If in Figure 13-11, 0-2 cannot shoot or pass the ball to 0-4 or 0-1 cutting to the basket he should dribble the ball out to the foul line extended. From this position he can pass the ball out to wing man 0-3,

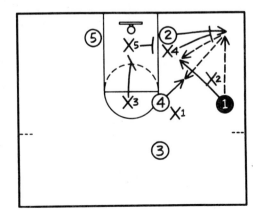

Figure 13-11

thus triggering our off-side series (Option 5) in the same manner as 0-1 did in Figure 13-7. Once the off-side series has been triggered, it will continue as illustrated in Figure 13-8.

PLAY 4: HIT THE PIVOT

The importance of passing the ball into the pivot has been discussed in great detail in some of the earlier chapters. The significance of the play is far greater when used in attacking a 1-2-2 zone defense than in any other type of zone defense we have experienced. Play 4, *Hit the Pivot,* is the best play we have in our basic six to attack the 1-2-2 zone. It has obtained its superior rating by enabling us, through its use, to isolate the baseline man on the strong side and set a screen on him as the ball moves over to the weak side.

Hit the Pivot has one big advantage over the other superior plays in our basic six series in that it enables us to attack the 1-2-2 zone defense in the middle, where it appears to be weakest. Once the ball is passed into the pivot, defensive adjustments must be made. Many times these adjustments cause weaknesses elsewhere in the defense. We work our point man and wing man long and hard in developing skills for passing the ball into the pivot. Our point man is asked to bring the ball down court so that he is in a direct line with pivotman 0-4 (Figure 13-12). From this position it takes just a short pass to get the ball into the pivot or into wing man 0-2. Point man 0-1 is asked to fake a pass to wing man 0-2 in an attempt to bait X-2 to move out and pick up 0-2. If X-2 moves out to defend our wing man, 0-1 will pass the ball to 0-4. If defensive man X-2 refuses to move out to pick up 0-2, 0-1 passes the ball to 0-2, who should have a drive opportunity, or he could fake a pass back out to 0-1, attempting to bait X-1 with picking up 0-1. If X-1 picks up 0-1, 0-2 can pass the ball into the pivot (Figure 13-13).

Play 4, *Hit the Pivot,* consists of the following four options:

Option 1: Hit the wing man cutting (Figure 13-14).
Option 2: Hit the off-side pivotman (Figure 13-14).
Option 3: Hit the point man (Figure 13-14).
Option 4: Hit the off-side wing man (Figure 13-15).

In Figure 13-14, 0-1 fakes a pass to 0-2, then passes to 0-4. 0-1 takes two steps toward the basket and then cuts off 0-4. 0-2 cuts back-door to the basket. 0-5 sinks to and rebounds the weak side. 0-3 moves

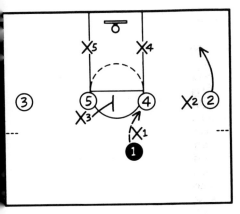

Figure 13-12

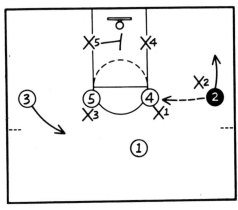

Figure 13-13

Figure 13-14

Figure 13-15

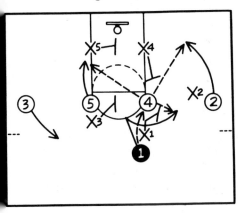

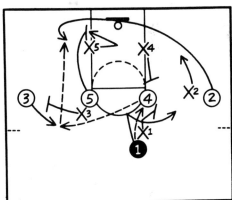

out to the top of the key. If defensive man X-4 moves out to defend 0-4, 0-4 passes the ball to 0-2.

If defensive man X-2 picks up 0-2 cutting, 0-4 should enter into Option 3 by hitting the point man.

If defensive man X-4 picks up 0-4, X-2 picks up 0-2, and X-1 picks up 0-1, then pivotman 0-4 enters into Option 4, hit the off-side wing man (Figure 13-15).

Here 0-2 after cutting to the basket clears to the opposite side behind 0-5. 0-4 passes to 0-3. 0-5 sinks to the basket, then sets a screen on X-5. 0-3 can pass to 0-2 coming off the screen, he can pass to 0-5 under or he can pass to 0-2 in the corner. If he passes to 0-2 in the corner, 0-3 can cut to the basket. If he does, the off-side series is entered into. If 0-3 passes to 0-2 and moves away from the ball toward the point, his actions will initiate the strong-side rotation series.

PLAY 5: THE DRIBBLE OVER

Play 5, the *Dribble Over,* is listed on our offensive rating chart as a superior play when used for attacking 1-2-2 zone defenses. The play is simple to execute. Considering its simplicity we often find it hard to believe that such a simple maneuver can affect zone defenses in the manner it does. Nevertheless, the play with its four options has proven to be successful one.

The four options of Play 5, the *Dribble Over,* are:

Option 1: Hit the off-side pivotman (Figure 13-16).
Option 2: Hit the on-side pivotman (Figure 13-16).
Option 3: Hit the off-side wing man (Figure 13-16).
Option 4: Pass the ball into the corner (Figure 13-16).

In Figure 13-16, 0-1 dribbles the ball over to the right wing position. 0-2 clears to the corner. 0-5 breaks to the low post on the strong side. 0-3 sinks to and rebounds the off side. 0-1 can pass the ball to 0-5, 0-4, 0-3, or 0-2.

Whenever point man 0-1 dribbles the ball toward the wing position, defensive men X-1 and X-2 are forced into making several quick adjustments. Considering that defensive man X-2 has the responsibility of defending against pivotman 0-4 as well as the wing position, X-2 must decide just when he should leave pivotman 0-4 unprotected to pick up 0-1 dribbling to the wing position. On the other hand, defensive man X-1 has the responsibility of defending 0-1 when the ball is out front as well as pivotman 0-4 when the ball is at the wing position. Both defensive men must make their adjustments as 0-1 is dribbling the ball. In the middle of their adjustments, pivotman 0-4 should be clear for an instant, and point man 0-1 should pass him the ball. When he does, he enters into Option 2, hit the on-side pivotman (Figure 13-17).

In this situation, 0-4 can shoot, pass to 0-5 under on the strong side, or pass to wing man 0-3 under on the weak side.

If defensive man X-4 picks up pivotman 0-4 and if defensive X-5 picks up 0-5 cutting to the weak side, point man 0-1 should pass the ball to wing man 0-3. With a pass to 0-3, point man 0-1 enters into Option 3, hit the off-side wing man. Wing man 0-3 should shoot the ball as 0-5 rebounds the weak side and 0-4 the middle.

If in Figure 13-16, defensive man X-4 picks up pivotman 0-4, point man 0-1 should pass the ball to wing man 0-2 who is left un-

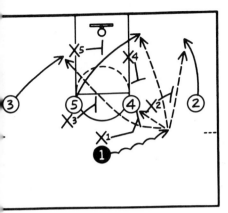

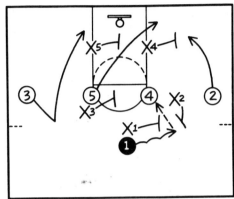

Figure 13-16

Figure 13-17

protected. With a pass to 0-2, point man 0-1 enters into Option 4, pass the ball into the corner.

Once wing man 0-2 gets the ball he should shoot. If for some reason, he cannot shoot the ball, he may be able to pass to 0-5 under or to 0-4 in the pivot. If both men are covered, wing man 0-2 should dribble the ball out and either enter into our strong-side rotation series (Figures 12-19 and 12-20) or our off-side series (Figure 12-21).

PLAY 6: THE DRIVE PLAY

Play 6, the *Drive Play* is listed as a superior play on our offensive rating chart in attacking the 1-2-2 zone defense for two reasons:

a. It adheres to the criteria we have set up for a superior rating.
b. In the event the zone defenses match up man-for-man, it is the best play in our offense.

The four options of Play 6, the *Drive Play* are:

Option 1: Hit the off-side pivot (Figure 13-18).
Option 2: Shoot or drive.
Option 3: Hit the on-side pivotman rolling to the basket.
Option 4: Hit the wing man.

In Figure 13-18, point man 0-1's pass to 0-5 is made possible by the defensive play of X-4. In order for 0-5 to be clear for a shot,

197

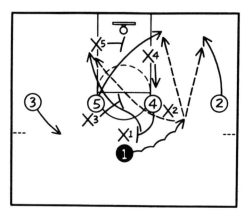

Figure 13-18

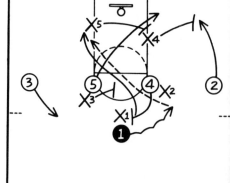

Figure 13-19

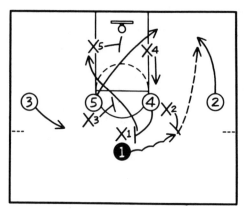

Figure 13-20

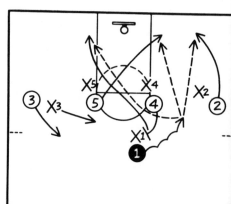

Figure 13-21

defensive man X-4 has to move away from his position under the basket. If he maintains his position, 0-1 can shoot, drive (Option 2), pass the ball to 0-4 rolling to the off side (Option 3), or pass the ball to 0-2 in the corner (Option 4). Point man 0-1 can pass the ball to pivot man 0-4 rolling to the off-side, provided defensive man X-5 moves away from his defensive position and picks up pivotman 0-5 (Figure 13-19).

If in Figure 13-19, defensive man X-5 picks up 0-4 and defensive man X-4 picks up 0-5 point man 0-1 should pass the ball to 0-2 in the corner (Option 4, Figure 13-20).

Play 6, the *Drive Play*, is the best play we have in our basic six to combat a match-up zone defense. For an opposing team to match up against the 1-4 offense, they must use a variation of the 1-2-2 zone defense. The match-up is illustrated in Figure 13-21. We will attack the defense in the same manner as we have outlined for attacking the 1-2-2 zone defense.

In Figure 13-21, 0-1, after receiving a screen from 0-4, has the same four options available to him as he had in attacking the 1-2-2 zone defense. He can pass to 0-4, 0-5, 0-2, shoot or drive to the basket.

This concludes our discussion of the 1-4 offense and the outline of our basic six against the various zone defenses. Although there are other types of zone defenses, we feel confident that our basic six will be as successful against them as they have proven to be against the 2-3, 1-3-1 and 1-2-2 zone defenses that we have already outlined for your consideration.

14

THE 1-4 OFFENSE

AGAINST PRESSURE DEFENSES

The game has changed. The game is changing. The game will change. Basketball is dynamic. Its future is hard for me to predict. I can, however, offer my views as to what I believe have been the major influencing factors for the changes past and present. In my opinion, the two greatest impacts on our game have been the jump shot and pressure defenses. I believe that pressure defenses have done for defensive basketball what the jump shot has done for offensive basketball. The magnitude of the impact may not have been to the same degree, but none-the-less pressure defenses have changed our game greatly. It's true that the jump shot has given the offense a permanent advantage over the defense and this, in my opinion, is as it should be. But pressure defenses are alert to this advantage and can, many times, cause the pendulum to swing the other way, particularly against ball clubs who are not adequately prepared to cope with this type of defensive play. It is our intention to offer for your consideration our 1-4 offensive attack against the following types of pressure:

1. The 1-4 against full-court zone pressure.
2. The 1-4 against full-court man-to-man pressure.
3. The 1-4 against half-court zone pressure.
4. The 1-4 against half-court man-to-man pressure.

The 1-4 Against Full-Court Pressure

There are several ways in which to successfully attack full-court pressure defenses. It is not our intention to discuss the merits of any of the others as compared to the 1-4. It is more important to us to make you realize the necessity of including in your offense some organized way of attacking pressure defenses than to sell you on our 1-4 attack. Even though there are a number of ways to go about attacking full-court zone defenses, whatever one you decide to use has to fall into one of two categories:

1.   Those attacks in which the basic premise is to get the offensive attack started before the defense has a chance to set up.

2.   Those in which the basic premise is more deliberate in nature and the idea is to attack the defense after it has been given a chance to set up.

Our 1-4 attack is a deliberate one. We wait for the defense to set up before we attempt to attack it. Furthermore, we use the same alignment against all types of full court pressure. It matters little if the defense is a full-court zone or a man-to-man. It makes little difference whether the full-court zone defense we are attacking is a 2-2-1, 1-3-1, or a 3-1-1; our alignment is always the same (Figure 14-1).

In our 1-4 alignment, 0-1 is usually our point man, and he takes the ball out of bounds. 0-2 and 0-3 are again referred to as the wing men and move to the positions indicated. Of the two wing men, 0-2 should be the better ball handler, passer, and dribbler. 0-4 and 0-5 are our pivotmen and usually play the positions outlined. Of the two pivotmen, the best ball handler, passer, and dribbler should occupy the position occupied by 0-4.

It is apparent here that we attack full-court pressure defenses with all five men taking part. From the outset let me warn you that most coaches believe such an alignment would never be able to do the job adequately. In rebuttal to these critics, we can only refer to the success we've experienced over the years. Furthermore, just as you have, we have experimented with various alignments. There can be only one reason why we use the one we do; obviously our attack has done the

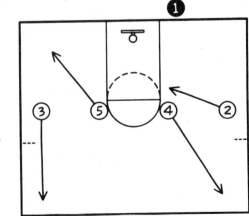

Figure 14-1

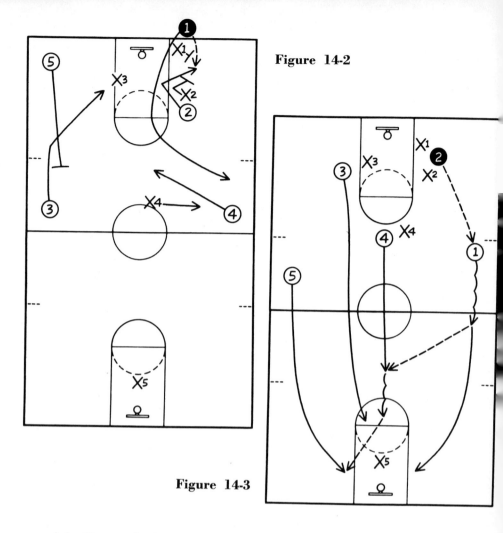

Figure 14-2

Figure 14-3

job. The method we use in attacking full-court zone defenses is referred to as the sideline. To illustrate the sideline method of attacking full-court zone defenses, let us outline the play against the 3-1-1 zone press (Figure 14-2).

In Figure 14-2, 0-1 takes the ball out of bounds. 0-2 fakes toward the free throw line, then breaks out to receive the ball. 0-5 screens down for 0-3. 0-3 breaks up to the free throw lane line and acts as our secondary outlet man. 0-1 passes to 0-2, breaks toward the foul line, and then angles to the sideline. 0-4, after 0-2 has received the pass in, breaks to the top of the key. Unless defensive man X-1 refuses to double up, wing man 0-2, after receiving a pass from 0-1, must not dribble the ball. He is a passer and can pass the ball to 0-1, his first choice; 0-4, his second choice; or 0-3, his third choice. 0-2's decision as to whom he passes the ball is determined by the defensive play of X-4 and X-3. 0-2 knows exactly where 0-1, 0-4, and 0-3 should be. He is instructed not to look at 0-1, 0-4, or 0-3. All his attention must be focused on the play of X-4 first and then on the defensive play of X-3. If defensive man X-4 picks up 0-4 breaking to the top of the key, 0-2 must pass the ball to his first choice, 0-1 (Figure 14-3). Once 0-1 is in possession of the ball he can:

1. Pass the ball to 0-4, who acts as the middle man on the fast break, and with 0-3 acting as a trailer 0-1 and 0-5 fill the fast break lanes (Figure 14-3).
2. Dribble to the middle and assume the middle position on the fast break with 0-3 acting as the trailer, 0-4 cutting behind him filling the left lane, and 0-5 filling the right one (Figure 14-4).
3. Dribble the ball down the sideline entering into a side fast break with 0-3 acting as the trailer, 0-4 filling the middle lane, and 0-5 responsible for filling the right lane (Figure 14-5).

Figure 14-4   **Figure 14-5**

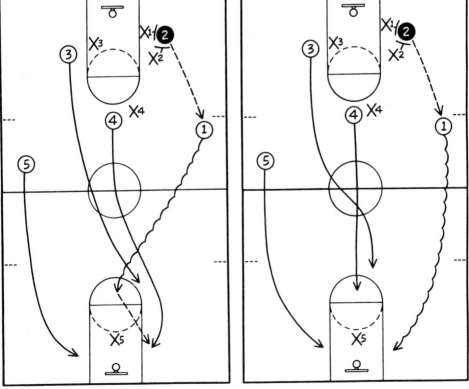

If in Figure 14-3, wing man 0-2 cannot pass the ball to 0-1, it can only be due to the defensive play of X-4. Defensive man X-4, instead of following 0-4 to the top of the key, moves to the side line either to pick up 0-1 after he receives a pass or to prevent him from receiving a pass. In any event, 0-2 should realize that X-4 has picked up 0-1. Once 0-2 realizes his first choice is unavailable, he looks to pass the ball to his second choice, 0-4 (Figure 14-6). Once 0-4 receives the ball, he passes the ball to 0-1 cutting. 0-1 now has the same three options available to him as he had in Figures 14-3, 14-4, and 14-5.

If in Figure 14-6 defensive man X-4 shuts off a pass to 0-1, 0-4 should look to pass the ball to 0-5 or 0-3. 0-4 can, if he is a good enough dribbler, dribble the ball down the middle and then become the middle man on the fast break.

If wing man 0-2 cannot pass the ball to point man 0-1 or to pivot-man 0-4, it can only be due to X-4 shutting off a pass into 0-1 and X-3, picking up 0-4 in the pivot. If such a situation exists, wing man 0-2 must pass the ball to his third choice, 0-3 (Figure 14-7).

Figure 14-6   Figure 14-7

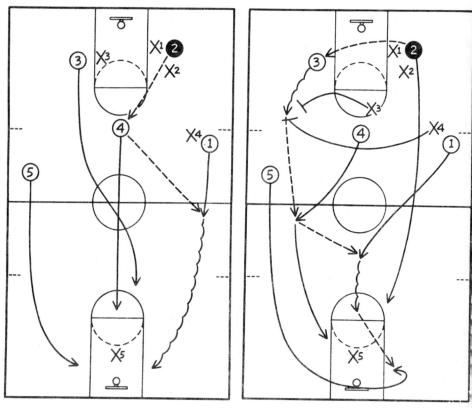

In Figure 14-7, once 0-3 receives the ball he must dribble the ball away from 0-2 until he is picked up by another defensive man. 0-5 breaks for the basket and fills the left lane. 0-4 breaks to the sideline beyond the mid-court line. 0-1 breaks to the middle. 0-2 acts as a trailer. As 0-3 dribbles the ball he looks to pass to 0-4. Once 0-4 receives the ball he looks to the middle for 0-1, passes him the ball, and starts the fast break. If 0-4 cannot pass to 0-1, he can dribble to the middle or dribble down the sideline in an attempt to get the break started.

If 0-3 cannot make his initial pass to 0-4, he can pass the ball to 0-1. 0-1 would then act as the middle man on the fast break.

The 1-4 Against the Full Court Man-for-Man Defense

We made the statement earlier that there are a number of good full-court zone pressing offenses available to coaches. All a coach must do is decide which one will suit his personnel best and then practice its execution; in most cases he will have an adequate attack. Consequently, because of the accessibility of a number of good offenses, the effectiveness of the full-court zone press has diminished markedly over the last few seasons.

Today, the full-court zone press is used primarily by a team that is behind on the scoreboard by a wide margin, or as a surprise defense geared to attack the offense for short periods of time throughout the course of the game. Basketball teams that use a full-court pressing defense as a full-time defense usually have included in their defense a full-court man-to-man designed to complement their zone. Ball clubs that are capable of employing both kinds of full-court defenses, changing from one to the other periodically, are very difficult for the offensive team to contend with. This is especially true of ball clubs that employ one separate offense for attacking full-court zone defenses and a completely different one for attacking full-court man-to-man defenses. Immediately, the need for a pressing offense that can successfully attack both kinds of defenses becomes apparent. We believe that the full-court offense we have just outlined for use against full-court zone defenses can also be used successfully against the man-to-man as well.

In Figure 14-2 we stated that wing man 0-2, after receiving inbounds pass from 0-1, should not dribble the ball unless defensive man X-1 refuses to double him up. What this statement implies is that wing man 0-2 can become a dribbler any time he is being defended by one man only. We adhere to the firm policy that for any basketball player to play on our team, he must be able to bring the ball up the court on a dribble one-on-one against one defensive man regardless of the defensive man's ability. To strengthen further our belief in such a policy we practice each of our players everyday on this phase of the game. We instruct them to bring the ball up court only with the intention of getting the ball across the mid-court line. The primary objective of the dribbler is not to beat his defensive man down court, but only to dribble the ball in such a manner that his defensive man cannot take it away from him or force him to stop altogether. The type of dribble we recommend is referred to by us as a protective dribble. We ask the dribbler to turn his back on the defensive man and dribble the ball up court. As he dribbles with his left hand, he must shuffle his feet in such a manner that his right foot is always in front of the left. Whenever he is forced to dribble towards his left, he must dribble right-handed and shuffle his feet in such a manner that his left foot is always in front of the right. Now that we have explained how we want our players to dribble the ball down court, let us diagram and explain how our pressing man-to-man offense attacks a full-court man-to-man pressing defense (Figure 14-8).

In this situation, wing man 0-2, after receiving a pass from point man 0-1, must determine the type of pressing defense being employed. He can make such a determination by analyzing the defensive play of X-1. If X-1 follows 0-1 to the side line, his action will indicate to 0-2 that the defense employed is man-to-man. Once X-1 follows 0-1 to the sideline, 0-1, 0-3, and 0-4 clear out so that 0-2 can dribble the ball up court one-on-one against defensive man X-2 (Figure 14-9).

In Figure 14-9, 0-2 dribbles the ball up court in the manner described earlier. Once he crosses the mid-court line and gets the ball near the front court, he initiates our man-to-man offense by executing one of the six plays diagrammed in the earlier chapters.

If in Figure 14-9, 0-2 is forced to pick up his dribble, he looks to pass the ball to 0-4. It is 0-4's responsibility to come out and get the ball whenever 0-2 has been halted.

The 1-4 Offense Against Half-Court Zone Pressure

As the popularity of the full-court pressure defenses has declined, the use of the half-court pressure defenses has shown a marked in-

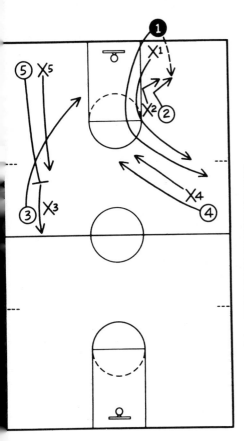

Figure 14-8

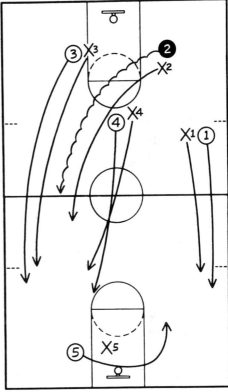

Figure 14-9

crease. I believe this is mainly due to the fact that half-court defenses are easier to play because there is less court area to defend and also because they are less strenuous on the players. Another good reason why the half-court pressure defenses are becoming more popular is the ease in which they can be concealed. Half-court pressure defenses make it possible for the defensive team to switch from a half-court zone to a half-court man-to-man and back again without much difficulty. Initially, most defensive teams make both types of defenses look the same, thus making it possible to conceal effectively the one they will actually play. This poses a problem to any team that uses a separate offense for attacking each of the two defenses. The two following solutions are effective in combating such concealed defenses:

1. Design one offense that can effectively attack both types of defenses.
2. Establish an effective means by which the particular defense to be used can be detected early, thereby enabling you to use two separate offenses.

In our 1-4 attack against half-court pressure we use two separate attacks, one for half-court zone pressure and a completely different one for use against half-court man-to-man defenses. Therefore, as we discussed earlier, we must have some means of diagnosing the defense to be used. This can be accomplished through the use of the offensive alignment we use for attacking half-court pressure defense as illustrated in Figure 14-10.

In Figure 14-10, as 0-1 is dribbling the ball up court, wing men 0-3 and 0-2 have the responsibility of detecting the type of half-court pressure defense they are confronted with. Wing men 0-2 and 0-3 are instructed to take the floor position as illustrated. Once they get over

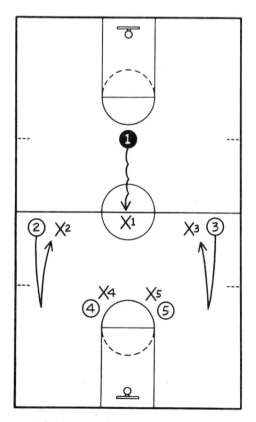

Figure 14-10

the mid-court line, they should take a few steps toward the foul line extended. If their defensive men follow them, 0-3 and 0-2 know immediately that they are confronted with a half-court, pressure man-to-man defense. Point man 0-1, by the actions of defensive men X-3 and X-2, is also made aware of the defense and consequently enters into our 1-4 half-court, man-to-man offense.

If in Figure 14-10, defensive men X-3 and X-2 hesitate and refuse to follow 0-2 and 0-3 to the foul line extended, their actions would indicate to 0-2 and 0-3 that the defense they are employing is a half-court zone press. Once the defense has been diagnosed, point man 0-1 enters into our 1-4 half-court zone offense. The half-court zone offense consists of the following three zone plays each of which has been presented in earlier chapters:

1. The corner play or sideline.
2. The weak-side series.
3. The pivot play.

Because of the manner in which they are used, plays 1 and 2, above should really be classified as one play only. Once the corner play is entered into, the off-side series follows. The off-side series for our purposes in this chapter is part of the corner play.

In our discussion of our 1-4 half-court zone offense we will present our attack against the 3-1-1 half-court zone press. In Figure 14-10, once defensive men X-3 and X-2 have committed themselves, 0-3 and 0-2 must return to the floor positions illustrated in Figure 14-10. These floor positions are so important that the entire success or failure of the pressing offense depends upon them. If 0-3 and 0-2 align themselves in a floor position that varies just a step or two from the position prescribed, the offensive team's chances of success are marginal. If 0-2 and 0-3 align themselves across from one another in a straight line with point man 0-1, the offense can beat the defense almost every time. The mistake most wing men like 0-2 make is to fade toward the basket whenever point man 0-1 has been trapped by defensive men X-1 and X-2. Whenever 0-2 fades toward the basket, he puts himself in a floor position where X-2 is between him and 0-1. Before 0-1 can pass the ball to 0-2, 0-2's floor position forces 0-1 to pass the ball through defensive man X-1. This is a very dangerous pass and can be easily deflected. If, however, 0-2 aligns himself in a straight line across from 0-1, 0-1 has a relatively safe and simple pass to make (Figure 14-11).

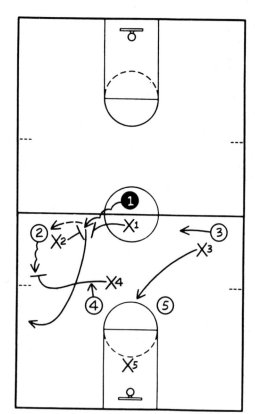

Figure 14-11

In this maneuver, 0-1 dribbles toward X-2, and when he is trapped, passes the ball to 0-2. 0-2 dribbles to X-4, the next defensive man. 0-1 cuts to the sideline eight or ten feet behind X-4 to serve as an outlet for 0-2. 0-3 moves to the center of the court. 0-4 takes two steps up toward the ball looking for a pass from 0-2. 0-5 maintains his position and watches the play develop.

Wing man 0-2 must dribble the ball to defensive man X-4. He must force X-4 to pick him up so that X-4 cannot defend 0-1 cutting behind him or pivotman 0-4 in the middle. Once defensive man X-4 moves over to defend 0-2, 0-2 picks up his dribble, provided he cannot drive to the basket, and looks to pass the ball to his first option, 0-4; 0-1, his second option; or 0-3, his third option.

If 0-2 passes to 0-4, 0-4 can shoot, drive or pass to 0-1 or 0-5 cutting to the basket or pass to 0-3 (Figure 14-12). If he passes to 0-3, 0-1 clears to the opposite side cutting behind 0-5; 0-5 sets a screen on X-5. 0-2 moves out to protect defensively and 0-4 rebounds the weak side (Figure 14-13). 0-3 can shoot, pass to 0-1 at the side of 0-5, pass

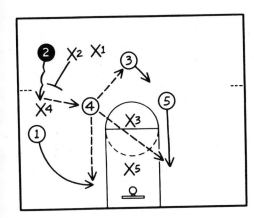

Figure 14-12

Figure 14-13

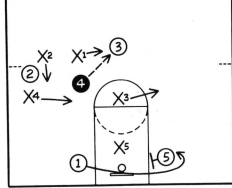

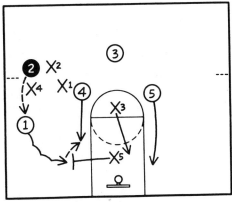

Figure 14-14

to 0-5 or pass the ball to 0-1 in the corner, which in turn triggers our off-side series.

In Figure 14-12, if 0-4 is defended, 0-2 looks to pass the ball to 0-1, his second choice (Figure 14-14). Once 0-1 receives the ball he dribbles to X-5, the next defensive man. 0-4 then cuts to the basket. 0-1 passes to 0-4 for a shot, or if X-3 is defending him, 0-4 can drop the ball off to 0-5 under.

If in Figure 14-14, 0-1 cannot pass the ball to 0-4 cutting to the basket, he looks to pass the ball back out to wing man 0-2. With such a pass 0-1 triggers our off-side series (Figures 14-15 and 14-16).

In Figure 14-15, 0-1, after passing to 0-2, clears to the opposite side, then after cutting behind 0-5, breaks out to receive a pass from 0-3. 0-2 passes to 0-3, then cuts to the basket. 0-3 dribbles the ball over toward the off side, and 0-4 and 0-5 watch the play develop.

In Figure 14-16, 0-2 clears to the off side, setting up next to 0-5. 0-5 screens X-5, 0-3 passes to 0-1, and 0-4 sinks to and rebounds the weak side. 0-1 has the same options available to him that 0-2 had in Figure 14-13.

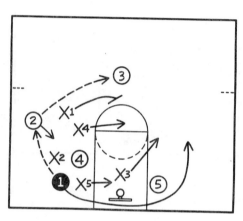

Figure 14-15

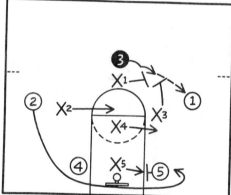

Figure 14-16

If in Figure 14-11, 0-4 and 0-1 are defended, 0-2 looks to pass the ball to 0-3, his third choice. With such a pass the off-side series is triggered. The responsibility of our players are the same here as they were in Figures 14-15 and 14-16. Many times in Figure 14-11, as point man 0-1 is dribbling the ball up court, defensive man X-4 gets careless, especially after we have run our sideline play a few times. In X-4's anxiety, pivotman 0-5 or 0-4 could be left undefended. Point man 0-1 must always anticipate X-4's movements, and once the pivot-men are clear, 0-1 must pass one of them the ball (Figure 14-17).

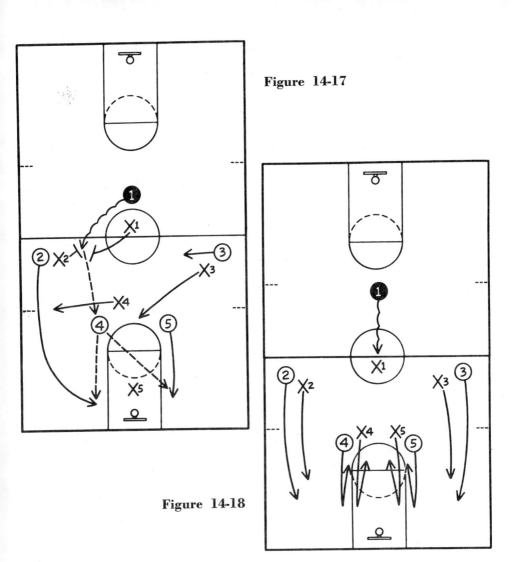

Figure 14-17

Figure 14-18

In Figure 14-17, if 0-4 passes to 0-5 or 0-2, they should shoot the ball. If 0-4 drives, his responsibilities are like those of a middle man on the fast break. If 0-4 selects to pass the ball to wing man 0-3, each player's responsibilities are the same as they were in Figure 14-13.

The 1-4 Offense Against Half-Court Man-to-Man Pressure

In Figure 14-18, point man 0-1 can enter into any one of the offensive man-to-man plays available to him, provided he can handle defensive man X-1. If defensive man X-1 is pressuring 0-1 extremely well, point man 0-1 may be forced to pick up his dribble. If so, it is the

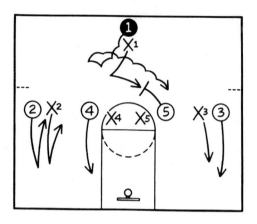

Figure 14-19

off-side pivotman's responsibility to come out and gain possession of the ball. Once the pivotman gains possession, the shuffle play is entered into. The entrance into the shuffle play in this manner has been outlined in Chapter 8 and it is not necessary to explain the play once again. In Figure 14-16, if 0-1's defensive man is pressuring 0-1 greatly, but not enough to force him to pick up his dribble, 0-1 can execute our *Go Play* (Chapter 8), or enter into a reverse dribble and drive off our off-side pivotman (Figure 14-19).

In Figure 14-19, 0-2 and 0-3 fade toward the corners clearing their defensive men away from point man 0-1; 0-4 and 0-5 sink toward the basket; 0-1 reverses his dribble and drives his defensive man off 0-5; 0-5 sets the screen, and 0-1 can drive to the basket, shoot, or pass to 0-3.

This concludes our discussion of the 1-4 offense against pressure defenses. Although our various offenses were diagramed against only one type of defense, the offenses presented are just as effective when used in attacking any of the other type of pressure defenses in use today.

INDEX